ALTERED COMPASS
EVIDENCE OF A BLACK IDENTITY CRISIS

Dallas T. Lee

Author's Tranquility Press
Marietta, Georgia

Copyright © 2022 by Dallas T. Lee

All rights reserved. No part of this publication may be reproduced, distributed or transmitted in any form or by any means, including photocopying, recording, or other electronic or mechanical methods, without the prior written permission of the publisher, except in the case of brief quotations embodied in critical reviews and certain other noncommercial uses permitted by copyright law. For permission requests, write to the publisher, addressed "Attention: Permissions Coordinator," at the address below.

Dallas T. Lee/Author's Tranquility Press
2706 Station Club Drive SW
Marietta, GA 30060
www.authorstranquilitypress.com

Ordering Information:
Quantity sales. Special discounts are available on quantity purchases by corporations, associations, and others. For details, contact the "Special Sales Department" at the address above.

Altered Compass/Dallas T. Lee
Paperback: 978-1-957546-97-1
eBook: 978-1-957546-98-8

Dedicated to Deron, Kayla, and David

Table of Contents

PART I 5
Directional Bearings 5
Withering Roots 11
My Child, Your Child 31
Where's Daddy? 47

PART II 76
The Calibration: Let's Talk 76
Education 78
Racism 84
The Science of Politics 101
A Response 110
My Concluding Thoughts 120
Your Reflections 125
ENDNOTES 129

ACKNOWLEDGEMENTS

There are a number of people who have challenged my thinking over the years in various ways. At times this challenge has been in the form of their willingness to listen to my thoughts and comments, and by doing so have allowed me opportunity to listen to myself. At other times, the challenge has come in the form of candid questioning of my perspectives, or by sharing their own valuable points of view. Whether their voice or mine, I have always tried to listen. Thus, I am forever grateful to my wife Karen. Your support is immeasurable—my world has balance because of you. Wanda Stevens and Michelle Davis, your encouragement and frequent thought provoking dialogue have meant more to me than you know. Mr. Denwood Barksdale, I sincerely thank you for your invaluable feedback, as well as reading, editing, and most of all, faith. I wish to thank Gwendolyn King, Tracy Rawls, and Theresa Tucker for honest input and feedback, and of course, knowing that God is. Gayle Hill and Anthony Gaston, thank you for your encouragement and taking a look when this manuscript was in its genesis—I remember.

Special Thanks to George Vallejo of Rancho Cucamonga, California for the initial cover design, and Al Desetta of New York for editing assistance.

Mom and Dad, because of you, this work is possible. Aunt Lola, your faith and courage is inspiring.

"My people are destroyed for the lack of knowledge."

Hosea 4:6

PROLOGUE

I first published Altered Compass in 2011. It was a consequence of conscious observations and experiences that informed me as a man of color, that an attitudinal and moral course correction is necessary, if we are to exist in a society in which life can be enjoyed with all being on an equal playing field, and in which we can be different, but respected and highly esteemed amongst ourselves, as well as by cultural others. In short, an existence in which life and lives are truly cherished.

Many events have transpired since that first publication, some being a continuation of happenings and trends already interwoven into the reality of our existence. Such as:

- The killings of men of color by men of color, as well as by those sworn to protect us.

- Challenges within the primary educational system.

- The increasing cost of obtaining a college education and rising student debt.

- The continuing and widening gaps between the haves and the have-nots.

- The ongoing change of the core family structure.

And other occurrences, that were unforeseeable. Such as:

- The Corona virus pandemic and its many effects on us not only as a deadly virus, but as a trigger of what is in my thinking, opinionated folly that has cost the lives of many.

- The BLM movement and the responses from various segments of society that reveals what are the views of that which is Black.

- The evolution of Face Book to "meta" and anticipation of what will be its impact on the developing and young minds of many.

- A Black female Vice President (will there be a backlash, such as following the administration of former President Obama?).

- The use of personal gender preferred identifiers, as to inform others of how you view yourself (male, female, other).

- And finally, the rise of Donald Trump and the many layers of political and social consequences that have followed, such as the resurgence of the overt racist, and the display of certain men and women in the political seats of power who make it clear that their hold onto power, over the rule of law, and the constitution, is the actual goal to be achieved and maintained.

Hence, the message of Altered Compass, is more relevant today than when it was first written.

PART I

Directional Bearings

As we in Black America proceed on the journey toward our future, what predominant perspectives will we carry from our past? Just as importantly, what common focal points will draw us onward as a people? In other words, what will be the shared views and collective visions shaping and influencing the destiny of tomorrow's "Blackness"?

For those of us whose ancestry, skin tone, facial features or hair texture, says "Blackness is my possession by birthright, mine by nature's assignment, and therefore mine to embrace and control," we, must strive to be a clear and illuminating voice in the process of interpreting and defining who we are as a people. We who understand our story must be the greater voice for all to hear, as opposed to those who do not intimately share in and live the Black experience, or those who hijack our identity and turn it into an ugliness which degrades the honorable people that we are. Hence, I beg the question: Do you, as I do, recognize the pressing need to collectively steer our course with greater determination in order to ensure the continuation of our noble legacy?

Ours is an amazing and still evolving saga. As a people we have faced many difficult challenges, improbable odds, and momentous obstacles, some of which have threatened our very survival. And yet, throughout our history, we have met those challenges, overcome those obstacles, and realized remarkable achievements due to our collective perseverance, unyielding effort, and self-defining purpose in spite of, what at times have been, daunting odds. In essence, our aim has typically been resolute action, as opposed to passivity and inaction.

In our present time however, I am noticing a mounting difference in how Black America responds to contemporary cultural, social, and political complexities. A difference that has its roots in an attitudinal transformation that has emasculated our once united socio-cognitive engagement, replacing it with a narrowly focused attention to self and an increasingly uncontested acquiescence to what are the systemic expectations of broader society.

If we respond to this attitudinal shift with indifference and an unquestioned acceptance of the status quo, we will be required to give up the idea of a brighter future for ourselves and the idea that collectively "we shall overcome." On the other hand, if shared values which honor life and determined action are to be our election, we will be engendered to turn a listening ear to our wise elders, as well as those who are, or have been, our civil rights soldiers, our exceptional educators and concerned spiritual leaders, as well as those graduates from the school of hard knocks, whose integrity, principles and morals have remained intact during this time of ethical decline and human struggle. We must listen to those who understand who they are, who recognize the importance of a moment, the worth of an opportunity, the advantage of self-discipline, and the irreplaceable significance of every human being's life.

At the same time, confronted by an extremely fast-paced digital age of increasingly advanced multi-media devices and services (laptops, mini-books, smartphones, ipads, twittering, facebook, blogging, tiktok, Instagram, and meta), it is imperative that we routinely and purposely tune out the incessant visual stimuli and auditory chatter made available to us, and with quietness, tune into our inner sanctums to spend purposeful time alone processing our private thoughts and pursuing conscientious insights. Only in this way can we more critically contemplate and comprehend the path that we collectively, and as individuals with eternal souls, are traveling. Indeed, as we move toward our personal and shared destinies, ours is a time that calls for sober introspection and spiritual reawakening.

For the Black community in particular, faith in God and the voices of prudent understanding have traditionally served as our initial points of departure for meaningful life experiences and vocation. I believe that faith and wisdom must once more become the launching points from which we plot our future course. In fact, it is the only proven course for uplifting and preserving a people who have been largely disregarded by the major decision makers and power wielders whose intentions have always been to control us, as well as the social and economic systems in which we live.

As we face our contemporary dilemmas, such as Black-on-Black crime, unstable families, a fragile economic climate, on-going racial divides, and the deteriorating behavioral and emotional conditions of many of our adults and children, I candidly ask, why would we allow the future direction of Black behavior and our interpersonal orientation to be continuously and increasingly determined by larger society's diminished values and principles, as opposed to reclaiming a renewed moral fortitude founded upon an internalized sense of unity that was once necessary for our very survival? What is happening to our psychological connection to one another and to our ancestors? Where is the mutual appreciation for one another's struggles?

Because of Black America's continuous process of assimilation, we are becoming increasingly less sagacious as a self-defining people; we lack a culturally focused, self-designed, and shared survival schema. In part, this is also due to the absence of a widely accepted and acknowledged base of contemporary Black leadership that projects a voice that uniformly captures a united vision, and hence, draws our allegiance and incites our energy. No people can successfully move with purpose from one point to another when their directional bearings are off balance and their world orientation is askew.

In whatever manner we choose to respond to the realities with which we are challenged to contend, I truly believe the words recorded in the book of Ecclesiastes, chapter 1 verse 9: "What has been will be again; what has been done will be done again; there is nothing new under the sun."[1] That is to say, within every personal and collective ordeal we face today, there is a correlated precedent. To every problem Black America faces, there is, if not a definite solution, at least a practical and constructive response—if we are courageous and honest enough to seek it. But to do so will require many of us to move beyond our respective comfort zones, as our capacity to solve our problems will hinge upon our readiness to face reality, and to then expend the necessary energy, faith, and integrity to engage our dilemmas in meaningful ways.

Unfortunately, it has become much more convenient and common for us to practice idleness, allowing unhealthy events and habits to govern our existence. As a result, many of our children and communities are trapped in a cycle of dire dysfunction.

As a Black mental health clinician, I will present my perspectives on harmful factors operating within the Black community that beg our urgent attention. I will also offer discourse regarding systems and practices within the larger society that appallingly affect all of our lives. Whether you agree or disagree with my analysis, I hope you will at least acknowledge the profound problems we face as a people and as a society. As you peruse the pages that follow, reflect on what I impart, speak to others, and together let us bring forth positive voices for change.

CHAPTER ONE

Withering Roots

> The night is beautiful
> So the face of my people.
>
> The stars are beautiful
> So the eyes of my people.
>
> Beautiful, also is the sun
> Beautiful, also, are the souls of my people.
>
> —Langston Hughes, "My People"[2]

Every human culture has its own functional wisdom and world view which are central to the health, survival, and identity of that people. This is what makes each ethnicity unique and enables divergent cultures to distinguish themselves from one another. However, once a particular culture's world view and traditional wisdom are lost, the people who comprise that culture also become lost, or, as in the case of extensive assimilation into another culture, they essentially become someone else. As Dr. Wade Nobles of San Francisco State University explains, "Thus the danger when one adopts uncritically the science and paradigms of another people's reality, is that one adopts their consciousness and also limits the arena of one's own awareness." [3]

Within the divergent cultural fabric of American society, Black America seems to be in an accelerated state of identity change, which appears to be occurring much quicker than in times past. Today, this change is progressively promoted and assisted by the tools of modern technology and media, and though the process of change is unavoidable, unchecked, unattractive or unhealthy change should not be viewed as desirable or acceptable. Though we continue to witness the intrinsic strength of Black character, resilience, and creativity by persons reaching the pinnacles of success in the fields of art, entertainment, sports, academia, and politics, we are also witnessing others who are too easily embracing behaviors and attitudes that demean not only the beauty of Blackness, but also the principled determination that has been entrusted to us by our foremothers and forefathers. I believe these behaviors and attitudes, at the very root, are the consequence of individuals psychologically buying into historically negative interpretations of "Blackness" that have been promoted initially by cultural others.

Today, as has been the case for centuries, we continue to contend with questions and negative depictions of who and what exactly is the "Black character". Without interruption, we discover persistent inquiry and what appears to be a shared uneasiness as regarding the estimation of those who are Black. This disconcerting reality holds true for most of us, which includes, as we have all witnessed, our 44th President of the United States. Consistent with the experience of many other Black men, Mr. Obama has incessantly dealt with negative portrayals and continuous questioning as to what he truly represents and who he is inwardly. In his case, the querying came to light when those attempting to keep him from gaining the presidential office played upon apprehensions within certain segments of the White population concerning men of color. After this initial strategy failed, the negative appraisals of his personality and political objectives served as an attempt to deflate and derail his presidential agenda. [4]

Damaging ideas about Blackness have their origins in cultural others' thought processes, which extend far back in history, beyond the African's enslaved presence on American soil.[5] Sadly, in this new millennium, in the most advanced and "civilized" society on earth, we find that unfair racial attributes, damaging adjectives, and stereotypical metaphors and similes remain connected to the idea of "Blackness". Unfortunately, vast numbers of people of color also blindly buy into these projections and notions, and in some cases even eagerly so. For example, we are often inundated today with the perennially detestable yet popular word "nigga".

As we know, "nigga" is derived from "nigger," the preferred expression of the racist when referring to a Black person who, in America, was once considered only three-fifths human. It is undeniable, that Black people have had, and continue to have, a deep psychological engagement with the word "nigger." [6] For some, and understandably so, this grappling has led to a conscious repulsion that is emotionally experienced through a process called "reaction formation," which takes the form of a phonic aversion. [7] This group, in response to their awareness and understanding of history, do not care to hear the "N" word in reference to themselves or to any others. The argument is that the word is patently distasteful and racially derogatory — period.

But there is another group that passionately claims the word "nigger" as their own, and zealously defends its usage. This group has sub-culturally redefined and mentally reframed the "nigger" concept, often changing the pronunciation of the word and intending its use, in most cases, to be a gleeful and benign greeting in reference to another Black, or in the clique White or other individual. Within this group, "nigger" or "nigga" always takes on a unique meaning based on the situation prompting its utterance.

"What's up, nigga?"

"That's my nigga!"

"Yo nigga."

And even when using the original pronunciation, as in "That nigger's crazy" or "We don't mess with them niggers," the word is readily understood and accepted by those who may just as aptly apply it to themselves within what they consider to be an acceptable context.

But the "N word" can become a real quandary for those of another ethnic makeup who have very little, if any, direct exposure to certain Black subcultures. Thus, ethnic others frequently fail to accurately understand the interpersonal depth and rhythm for the word's usage because they are psychologically removed from personally identifying with it. Their only clear-cut internalized comprehension of the term "nigger" is as it's actually intended to be understood from the racist mindset. Thus, they can never really grasp an affable, broader encompassing use for the word, and consequentially, they can never conceive of applying "nigger" to themselves in any capacity. The way in which those within this group simply say the word, regardless of its intended use, often comes off being offensive.[8] Nonetheless, each of us who are Black must realize that irrespective of how you verbally pronounce or employ its use, the "N" word was crafted for us, by small-minded individuals; not crafted by us. Indeed, the word is patently distasteful and racially derogatory — period.

In addition to the ways we speak about ourselves, some of us have so absorbed Western ideals that even when it comes to what is physically desirable and attractive, we gravitate toward what European tradition considers being beautiful and eye-catching. Take the Black celebrity or professional athlete, whose star status immediately breaks down traditional cross-cultural mating barriers. These individuals often seek the cultural other for dating, mating, and marriage; some strictly so.

Presently, it is not uncommon to see Black people sporting blue-colored contact lenses and wearing weaved-in or dyed straight blond or bleached hair, not to mention the skin lightening procedures pursued by some.[9]

These examples speak to mental conditioning that begins early in life resulting in damaged egos and inadequate self-images; a diminished sense of self-worth that is exacerbated by an obsessive psychological connection to, and need to emulate, those who are self-presumed to be closer to the ideal. Otherwise, why would some of us be compelled to transform our features to appear less Black or stringently pair sexually with someone outside the race? This can only lead to a further loss of Black identity and to culturally "selling out." Altering one's appearance or mating with a cultural other, depending on the motivating factors, points toward a disregard for our unique physical beauty and the potential for emotionally rewarding Black-on-Black relationships. And though I realize that love and natural attraction transcends one's race, my criticism arises when the underlying cause for cultural crossover, whether through changing one's appearance or selecting a mate, is steeped in reasoning that denies the innate beauty and potential of that which is Black.

In spite of the many advances in positive self-image attained during the "Black Movement" of the 60s and early 70s, we can daily witness highly destructive activities seeping into our intra and inter personal lives to such a degree, that there is now a thuggish, sexually permissive, Black exploitive image being presented as us, to us, by us! These distorted images of Blackness perpetuate and further create stereotypes in the minds of casual observers, but more importantly, contaminate the developing minds of Black youth. For example, the modern "gangsta" image and subculture dismisses the noble moral stratum that has long represented the historical content of our character. It mocks the fortitude and avid spirit Black people heroically displayed while in the midst of the most oppressive condition of human existence (chattel slavery), and during the long period of civil rights struggle that followed and continues today.

More than a few of our self-promoted descriptions and visual images are racially debasing and damaging to our identity. When objectively considered, many are quite absurd and some rather caricature in quality. In fact, we must examine "caricature" a bit closer, as both depictions of appearance and speech is part of our current entertainment culture. For example, take the night time cable cartoon series "The

Boondocks." In this series we often see young Black males with their pants sagging so low that their underwear are almost entirely exposed. There they are, in animation just as in real life, swearing for all within earshot to hear, verbally referring to one another and others as nigger, baseball caps angled to the side (some revealing wave caps underneath), wearing oversized sports jerseys or tight fitting "wife-beaters." Many sport expensive and unlaced "Flavs" (Nikes) or Timberland boots, while smoking "black-and-mild" cigars. To see these individuals strolling along in real life is interesting, but to see them moving quickly or attempting to run is actually comical (caricatures in motion). Nevertheless, for many of our youth, the "thugged out," "hip-hop," or "gangsta" presentation is stylish young Blackness, so prevalent that even White and other ethnic groups attempt to mimic it.

The rap music industry, movies and magazines have extensively popularized and promoted this particular way of dress along with accompanying language style and mannerisms. Of course, the gansta lifestyle may not truly represent the individual sporting the look, but most observers are not interested in asking questions and seeking answers about the individual's true character. The casual observer simply interprets the image as truth.

When a White, Hispanic, or Asian youth exhibits the thuggish or gangsta" appearance, many are likely to perceive him or her in a negative fashion, while others will simply conclude that he is "acting Black". That is, portraying style, movements, and verbal idiosyncrasies identified as having prominent expression in Black street culture. However, for the White or minority youth who can claim a racial identity other than Black, and easily be perceived as such, a change of clothing style along with verbal realignment with mainstream articulation will typically produce a much improved impression of character from the observer. Conversely, for the Black youth, many onlookers will remain suspicious of him even if he changes his sartorial style and grows beyond the gansta or hip-hop manner of speech and swagger. The likelihood is that the observer's negative impression and suspicion of the Black child will continue far beyond his youthful years. Even so, one's behavioral presentation, and appearance, should not provide an easy pretext for uncomplimentary thoughts by others. If negative impressions are formulated by the Black presence, it should simply bring to light an observer's speculative distortions and/or stereotypical biases unrelated to reality. However and regrettably, even as adults, too many of us fail to mature beyond adolescent attitudinal displays and manners of communicating; hence, the onlooker recurrently feels vindicated when holding onto generalized negative notions. How frequently do you see 30- and 40-year-old men and women apparently stuck in a juvenile stage of life, dressed in hip-hop fashion and running from the responsibilities of adulthood? Or witness mothers talking to their young children employing obscenities first used when talking to their adolescent peers? Mind-bogglingly, when the Black individual matures, enunciates words and phrases clearly without the use of colloquialisms, and strives to become studious, he or she is said to be acting White when observed by some Blacks!

Why hold on to behavior that is universally undignified, or permit our youth to pair themselves with what is clearly recognized as deleterious visual imagery and speech? In terms of imagery, some clothing lines even make it convenient for the preschooler to dress in a thugged out, hip-hop flair. Essentially grooming the child, with the parent's cooperation, to embrace an identity that will only increase the height of ongoing hurdles that he already has to overcome in life.

It is indeed unfortunate that so many of us, through our attitudes and actions work so diligently to comply with stereotypes and all the more so, advance negative models of who many perceive us to be. Hence, we cannot honestly voice surprise at the creation, a number of years ago, of a board game entitled *Ghettopoly*, which brazenly twisted Blackness into being represented by dope, sex, and crime. This board game, produced by an individual seeking to make a profit at our expense, was actually being sold on the shelves of Urban Outfitters until Rev. Jesse Jackson, Rev. Al Sharpton, and Kweisi Mfume protested its production and marketing. [11] Needless to say, until it was pulled from the shelves, this culturally debasing board game was being sold like hot cakes.

I wonder how many *Ghettopoly* players found it amusing as they failed to make any progress around the game board because of self-defeating illicit pursuits, which served as the game's actual obstacles to progress. But the more relevant question is this: How many amuse themselves in response to our self-defeating practices and endeavors in real life? How tragic. Deeper still, is that so many of us choose to spend our own money on self-degrading commodities of "entertainment" that create wealth for CEOs laughing behind the scenes, irrespective of their race or color.

Today, if Bitch, Ho, Nigga, Gansta, Thugging, Sexing, Hustling, Pimping or other pejorative insinuations aren't included in the visual images, musical lyrics, or literature (fictional or otherwise), it "ain't selling" to a large segment of us. Look at the promoted and popular fictional books written by a preponderant number of Black authors in any major bookstore. Something's amiss. Far too many of us have an overwhelming attraction to titles and illustrative content that suggest some form of vice or sexual impropriety. This is extremely revealing, because it so aptly speaks to a flawed life orientation that diminishes the ethical quality of our existence. The results are readily seen in many existent lives: low self-esteem, confused and chaotic interpersonal relationships, underachievement, absent fathers, promiscuity, depression, endemic anger, incarceration, and premature death.

When considering this reality, I have repeatedly asked myself, "How can this occur within a culture that produced individuals such as David Walker, W.E.B. Du Bois, James Weldon Johnson, Harriet Tubman, Nikki Giovanni, Langston Hughes, Malcolm X, and the man who boldly proclaimed the profoundly timeless and visionary "I Have a Dream" speech?

As I have considered our present plight, I have frequently allowed myself to vividly imagine how an aged Dr. Martin Luther King Jr., and Malcolm X, both very elderly, gray, and perhaps balding, would converse if they were alive and sitting at the table of dialogue earnestly sharing insights during Obama's presidency and about some of our contemporary predicaments and practices.[12]

Dr. King: "You know, Brother Malcolm, I have always been amazed by our people's resiliency and perseverance, which allowed us to confront the ugliness of old Jim Crow and those other schemes of our oppressors, at a time when only a very few of us were college educated and most didn't have two cents to spare."

Dr. King pauses, gazing somewhere beyond Malcolm.

"Yet, I have long felt uneasiness for my race deep down in the bowels of my spirit, because I clearly recognized that the powers that be, which we so desperately tried to reform, would counterattack and implement the right strategy to hamstring us at our weakest points."

Malcolm removes his eyeglasses and leans forward, pointing a slightly trembling finger and nodding in agreement.

Malcolm: "Yes, Brother Martin, our points of weakness! But who can dispute the fact that we clearly demonstrated within our communities, and to a narrow-minded governmental system, that steadfastness in unity, purpose, and endeavor, can achieve, at a personal, national, and international level, that which some deemed impossible."

He pauses, absorbed by a relevant memory from the past.

"But I too sensed, starting in the late 1970s, that there was a different mindset evolving within our race. That feeling of togetherness that we had here at home and were beginning to gain in the international community, that perception of unison with our African and other nonwhite brothers and sisters—yes, that appreciation of cohesive purpose—was subtly on the decline. And indeed, that the age old strategy, 'divide and conquer,' was being planned and orchestrated in places too high and exclusive for a 'real Black' person's access."

Malcolm shakes his head.

"You know, even today, some 40 years after the movement, it's amazing how many people share the conviction that Obama doesn't belong in the 'White House' because he's a 'Black Man.' We must support that brother, and yet, hold him rigorously accountable to govern for the middle and lower classes! The wealthy have received governing favoritism for far too long now."

Dr. King: "Yes, it is our duty to not only support him, but to hold him to the tow. But with the callous mindset that so many of our people possess today, we will potentially cheat him out of the support he deserves. We will cheat him, as well as those others standing in the wings with potential political ascension. Yes, and we will certainly cheat ourselves if we fail to take advantage of the opportunity to speak up and stand for positive change regardless of who is in the presidential office. Indeed, we have been hamstrung, Brother Malcolm."

Dr. King leans forward.

"Hamstrung at our weakest points—knowledge and communal fortitude! Just as with you, Brother Malcolm, the source of my chronic distress has been and continues to be our loss of spiritual kinship, and how so many of our youth, especially our young Black males, have developed an aversion toward education and intellectual enlightenment, the very key to expanding one's horizons and realizing astonishing potential!"

"Yes, Malcolm, as you say, I have sensed this change since the late 1970's, when the power of togetherness faded and the energy of disunity started to gain momentum. It was the time when we went from Afro-Sheen to curl activator, and from Dashikis and Brooks Brothers to 'Members Only.' But the degree of it! I never dreamed that after the harmony I witnessed down in Birmingham . . ."

Dr. King briefly pauses as he recalls events from the past.

". . . that after the purpose and pride displayed in sweltering Selma or the soul refreshing fellowships on Sunday mornings at Ebenezer, that we as a people would become so disillusioned and divided!"

Malcolm: "Indeed, the right strategy was implemented! Just keep robbing the identity and quenching the communal pride. Talk about mis-education of the Negro! It's all about the material now, and little about morals, principles, intellectual aptitude, togetherness, or the spiritual. It's all superseded by the material!"

"How many brothers and sisters today would stop using a public service or product to send a socially relevant message to the powers that be? Especially if doing so meant jeopardizing a job, not to mention bleeding? Yet one Black man, without the slightest hesitation, will draw blood from another Black man because he wants the little that the other has. Or more incomprehensible still, because one wears red while the other wears blue, when both are Black! Black!"

"We who are Black, the strongest color in the spectrum, the sum total of all colors! We who are Black maim and kill one another over lesser colors exhibited on beads, belts, and bandanas!"

Malcolm reclines back in his chair, visually disturbed. But then, after a moment, he smiles.

"You know, if our people had the same spirit of unity and visionary vigilance that we possessed back in '63', the American pie would have a much richer chocolate filling by now. I even believe that with the activists you drew to your marches and those I attracted to my rallies, that we, with the rest of America, could even get today's gas prices back down to 50 cents a gallon."

Malcolm chuckles.

"Well, perhaps I exaggerate."

Dr. King: "Fifty cents? 50 cent! How would our community have responded to him back in . . ."?

He lets the thought go, then smiles and shakes his head before getting back on topic.

"You're forgetting about those eight deceptive years, with old Cheney and Bush recklessly holding the reigns of a nation! Those scoundrels and their cohorts really did a job on us. Our present state-of-the-nation is the result of their highest priorities—ensuring increased wealth for the wealthy, and profiting from petroleum products beneath the Middle Eastern desert! Yes, the stuff upon which this nation depends—money and oil, or perhaps I should simply say greed, that thing for which our young soldiers, along with the less advantaged populations of other countries, are paying the ultimate price. I would have loved to have gotten Cheney and Bush into a few of my morning worship services back when their characters were still forming. I would have preached up a hailstorm, then maybe . . ."

Malcolm laughs and interrupts.

Malcolm: "What? Brother Martin, now don't underestimate the profound influence I myself could have made, because there was a time when I could have talked those then young rascals into eating bean pies and wearing kufus!"

Visualizing the image, the two share laughter.

"No, no. On second thought, I had my limitations."

More laughter, followed by a long and reflective pause.

Dr. King: "You know, Brother Malcolm, we both had our limitations, but so much of what we are seeing in our up and coming generations is far removed from what we tirelessly promoted. You know, it seems that so many of our people have become disconnected from their roots."

Malcolm nods in agreement and closes his eyes.

Malcolm: "I know what you mean, Brother Martin, and as time passes those roots increasingly wither. Yes, Brother Martin, I know exactly what you mean."

Malcolm speaks almost in a whisper.

"How long can something survive, disconnected from its roots?" [13]

* * *

Modern life seems to move so rapidly, with scores of us entrenched in trying to make it, get ahead, or just get by, that we do not adequately reflect upon or process our behaviors, perceptions, and belief systems from an ethical and spiritual perspective. There is always some new and multifarious information demanding our attention and needing to be immediately dealt with. As a result, we too often lack a healthy interpersonal orientation, communal temperament and consciousness of the divine. Hence, many of us simply fall into a rhythm that works best at protecting what little comforts we have or are working toward. We then saunter on, to the next moment, hour, day, week, and years. At least until events take place that are so appalling and shocking that they compel us to question, if only briefly, what's really occurring around us.

On February 9, 2010 many of us watched the television news in disbelief, as a Seattle transit surveillance camera recorded a 15-year-old Black teenage girl being maliciously attacked by a group of her female peers.[14] The same camera captured three Black adult security guards standing idly by, emotionally detached as they witnessed the assault. They reportedly chose not to intervene because their job descriptions required them only to "observe the activity" in the tunnel.[15] Similar situations, in which adults fail to act on behalf of children have since been reported and caught on camera.[16]

It is hard to imagine that two or three generations ago, Black adults would not have stepped in to provide assistance to a Black child or any child in distress, no matter what their job descriptions instructed them to do or not do. How did we get to the point of failing to help someone who is in imminent danger or trouble? What is occurring within our psyches to cause such diminished compassion for one another? Who and what are we becoming?

Today there is a fraying of our emotional connection with others, an interpersonal disconnect that often increases as those "others" become further removed from our family of origin or core social circle.[17] For some, this disconnect is all inclusive and can become nearly impossible to reverse. Individuals with such emotional orientations, at minimum, have an unhealthy way of interacting with the world around them, while others can become extremely dangerous and destructive. Let's consider the extreme.

The Washington, D.C. sniper shootings of 2002 are an unsettling example of the potential harm done when the interpersonal disconnect is combined with anger and serious moral slippage. John Allen Muhammad, who was executed by the Virginia Judicial system in October 2009, and Lee Boyd Malvo, now serving a life sentence without parole, committed the shootings.

Before these two were arrested, none of us, of whatever race or ethnic group, suspected Black men to be remotely involved. During the nightly news reports, the most experienced and esteemed criminal profilers missed the mark on who the "likely perpetrator" was, as the murdering rampage of Muhammad and Malvo continued. This is understandable, because random and serial killings have not typically been a part of Black Americans' behavior, male or female, regardless of the degree of anger or emotional dysfunction involved.[18]

Nevertheless, as I have reflected upon these senseless and savage shootings, I have had to consider whether in fact, the Western mindset, which has historically promoted excessively heartless behavior and is increasingly amoral, plays a major contributing role in grooming the mentality for a merciless interpersonal disconnect to flourish. So the question becomes, "Is the Western cognitive influence in essence, evidenced in Muhammad's and Malvo's actions?"

At first glance, this question may seem a bit farfetched or absurd, but disregarding the humanness of the individual and collective others has been a long tradition within Western thinking. From a historical view, we must note an almost complete eradication of the American Indian from American soil. As well, we are compelled to witness the early creation of deplorable conditions and enslavement of Blacks for selfish gain. We are also required to acknowledge the dropping of two atomic bombs on a foreign population on the island of Japan, not to mention the continual exploitation of peoples around the globe for egocentrically driven purposes. It is clear, that the communal Western way of thinking says: overpower, grab, take, control, and if need be eliminate. For the more unstable individual, this orientation can become dangerously personal when relational inadequacy or a self-presumed capacity to obtain something desperately desired is lacking or in some way inhibited; i.e., loss of a job, relationships, inability to make tenure[19], as well as persistent annoyance due to certain life events. Frustration may then be indiscriminately turned outward towards that which is least valued, that is, other human beings. Interestingly, we notice that random and serial killing has usually been committed at the hands of a disgruntled White psychopath who feels powerless or wronged in some way.[20]

In the case of the D.C. sniper shootings, practically everyone thought the perpetrator was either White or foreign born. What a surprise when the faces of two apprehended Black men flashed across America's television screens. Later investigation revealed that John Muhammad, the duo's leader, was extremely discontented with his personal circumstances.

Let's consider. African-Americans typically commit crimes within the perimeters of their own neighborhoods in the form of robbery, drug use, or drug distribution. When the crime becomes violent, it is often the consequence of a soured relationship, or because something deemed disrespectful was directly said or done. Black, and Black-on-Black crime typically speaks to the diminished degree of worth some within our race place upon themselves and others with pigmented skin. The depleted regard they ascribe to Blackness results in victims and victimizers within the race, albeit with the consequence being that lives are too easily ruined or taken. Even still, we have not normally perpetrated purposeful acts of random killings. Although, as evidenced in the above case and the one that follows, this appears to be changing.

On August 3, 2010, Omar Thornton, a Black truck driver for a beer distributor in Connecticut, was asked to resign his job or face termination after being caught on video footage stealing from the company.[21] Omar was a disgruntled employee who reportedly had complained to his Caucasian girlfriend that he had experienced racial harassment on the job that was never resolved.[22] After signing his resignation papers, he randomly shot and killed eight fellow employees before fatally wounding himself.

Though the daily pressures and demeaning social subjugation that Blacks have experienced and continue to endure in American society, has perhaps only been surpassed at one point in history, by the American Indian, we have—

surprisingly—withstood life's repeated blows without lashing out with random violence at the broader community. Our ego strength has traditionally enabled us to press on in the face of our immediate situations and conditions. At worst, the more emotionally pained and damaged individuals within our race, as mentioned above, victimize those with whom they have had some dealings or intimate interactions, again, usually within the confines of their own geographical locations; a ruinous dynamic within itself. But what John Muhammad masterminded and how Omar Thornton responded to his job termination were on a completely different plane, definitely beyond our diachronic interpersonal response style to an emotional breakdown, loss of employment, feelings of rejection, or of even being hated by society in general. Hence, an essential and honest inquiry is, "Do the cases of John Muhammad and Omar Thornton suggest that we are experiencing a much deeper psychological merging with Western ways and culture than in the past?" As well, "Is our assimilation within this increasingly amoral and violent society priming more John Muhammads and Omar Thorntons?" And finally, "Are we witnessing a fundamental mental shift that normalizes a heartless emotional disconnect from our fellow human beings, resulting in destructive interpersonal dynamics, which are bound to follow?"

I venture to say that the answers are "yes," unless we reclaim the moral and spiritual roots that have served as our social and interpersonal compass in times past.

CHAPTER TWO

My Child, Your Child

The Masai warriors of Africa have traditionally greeted each other by asking the question "Kasserian ingera?" Which means, "And how are the children?" This inquiry is made because the well-being of the children is considered to be an accurate barometer for the well-being of the tribe.[23]

Regardless of the socioeconomic circumstances and environment a child is born into, that child is born innocent. Yet, without question, external conditions soon begin to shape his or her behavioral, moral, emotional, and intellectual development. In essence, who and what is available in one's environment directly affect the child's perceptions, eventual overt activities, and life outcomes. In the field of psychology, this is understood as social learning.[24] What is continually modeled for the child at the various stages of development becomes ingrained within the child's mind, significantly influencing the decision-making and behavioral pattern that will be exhibited for years to come.

Consider the case of Michael Vick, the extremely talented Black professional football athlete with nothing but more money to make and NFL records to break.[25] I must admit that I was a long-time fan of Mr. Vick, since his days at Virginia

Tech, and I am immensely excited about his incredibly impressive comeback and the mental strength that he exhibited. His personal resilience, as well as skills on the playing field, is amazing. Nevertheless, I must offer him here as an illustration, because he so clearly represents the point of my argument.

In what has become a significant episode in his professional career, Mr. Vick engaged in a vice that is admittedly popular with a number of inner-city youth and adults, though its popularity stretches far beyond the inner city.[26] Certain peers and associates within Vick's community reportedly exposed him to dog fighting at an early age. Years later, after his athletic skills had propelled him out of the "hood" and onto a course of stardom and financial security, Vick chose to be the financial underwriter of a dog fighting enterprise prefixed by the term "Bad Newz," in his hometown of Newport News, Virginia. To the chagrin of many of his fans, one of Michael Vick's early environmental impacts surfaced in his adult preoccupation with an illegal activity.

Here was a grown man who, if animal sport were his passion, had enough money to breed, raise, train, and race world-class racehorses. Instead, he bred pit bulls to fight and kill other pit bulls, as part of an ill-conceived and relatively small-time hustle. If Vick's dark obsession had gone undiscovered, who knows how long his dog fighting "business venture" would have lasted? The effects of social learning that had not been duly unlearned lay at the core. But his foible was discovered and, as we all know, he spent 19 months incarcerated in a federal penitentiary and many hours reeducating himself regarding the humane treatment of animals. And so, once more with fortitude and perceptive planning, he is set to prevail. Even still, in-spite-of how well he performed on the playing field during the 2010 football season, sports commentators were often compelled to mention his crime and sentence during game time.

(As an afterthought, there didn't appear to be as much mention, during league games, of Steelers quarterback Ben Roethlisberger being twice accused of sexual assault, or quarterback Brett Favre allegedly sending lewd photographs to a female over his cell phone. I wonder what their childhood environments and circumstances consisted of?)

* * *

In 1930 John B. Watson (1878-1958), the founder of behavioral psychology, hypothesized that behavior is shaped by experience and stated:

> Give me a dozen healthy infants, well formed, and my own specified world to bring them up in and I'll guarantee to take any one of them at random and train him to become any type of specialist I might select—doctor, lawyer, artist, merchant, chief, yes, even beggerman and thief—regardless of his talents, penchants, tendencies, abilities, vocations, and race of his ancestors.[27]

Though Watson qualified his statement as being an exaggeration, he also spoke with a degree of sincerity based upon the scientific analysis and behavioral observations of his day. If Watson was able to posit such a hypothesis in 1930, then we are in dire need of asking serious questions about the "specified worlds" in which we are rearing our children today. It is very clear that immense populations of our young people possess mindsets and behavioral practices that are dangerously dysfunctional. It is also becoming more and more evident that for American children in general, their grave dysfunction is surfacing at earlier and earlier ages. [28]

Let's go back some years. In April 2008, there was an alarming story in the headlines involving young children in Georgia suspected of plotting the murder of their third-grade teacher.[29] Upon being exposed, they had in their possession a steak knife, a crystal paperweight, a set of handcuffs, and a roll of duct tape. During the summer of 2009, the headlines reported a 15-year-old Florida male being doused with rubbing alcohol and set afire by peers in a dispute over a bicycle.[30] In April 2010, a 14-year-old boy called 911 after intentionally shooting and killing his father. When asked why he shot his dad, the boy replied that he didn't know.[31] On August 1, 2011 we read, "3 Siblings Arrested After High-Speed Chase, Shootout."[32] This headline announced three teenaged persons, two males and a female, who had gone on an interstate robbery and shooting spree. When finally apprehended they were found to have two AK-47 machine guns, a machine pistol and a hand gun in their possession. The female in the group was shot in the leg after she raised her pistol towards an officer of the law during her final effort to escape capture. And then on August 11, 2011 it was reported, "17-year-old Student Planned In Advance to Kill Principal."[33] The news event following this caption made known the stabbing murder of a school principal by a seventeen year old adolescent who harbored resentment because of a class change mandated by the principal the previous school year.

Such reports involving children and teenagers committing serious delinquent acts and vicious crimes are no longer infrequent. Hence, our social paradigms must be soberly examined for the effects they are having on our children's minds and behavior.

Thus, we need to raise relevant questions, explore the validity of all possible answers, and let the chips fall where they may. However, we must also go a step further. We must be mature enough as a society to pursue real and practical solutions, and it is imperative to start at the family and community level.

We must sincerely consider why so many of our children fail to develop respect for authority, form healthy relationships with the opposite sex, realize their true potential, and grow beyond the stage of childish entitlement. We must also consider the factors related to them developing and maintaining deep-seated levels of anger, aggression, rebellion, low self-esteem and diminishing self-respect. We must address, within the Black community and society at large, why staggering numbers of youth, especially Black youth, end up incarcerated, and the reasons this phenomenon is often repeated over generations. We must address the causes of why gang culture has become so popular and attractive to our children, and for the degree of multigenerational gang enmeshment often found in immediate and extended family systems; systems that set the very trajectory of a child's life.[34] And for certain, it is time we respond with integrity to what leads our children to become parents before they've had the opportunity to develop into responsible and mature adults themselves; adults with an understanding of what constitutes good parenting skills and family stability.

To effectively respond to such profound issues, and develop reasonable conclusions and suitable remedies, will require painful honesty. As well, we must set aside our collective denials and free ourselves from being held mentally hostage by those "experts" who purport solutions that dismiss, minimize, or dissuade us from considering the legitimacy of common sense, traditional wisdom and practices; otherwise, real solutions will remain elusive and difficult to discover.

It doesn't take much, other than perceptual acuity and candor, to recognize that many of our modern-day methods and ideologies have contributed to the progressive deterioration of our young people's emotional maturation, loss of magnanimity, and fledgling responsible behavior. Hence, by objectively considering the dilemmas facing our youth, we will be obligated to admit that it is we adults who have essentially shaped their behavior through ever-increasing permissive interactions and developmentally damaging parental practices, which include:

- Giving our children "everything" we did not have.

- Exposing our children to visual images and language that accelerate their subjective impressions of being "grown up," before they have the opportunity to actually grow up.

- Believing it is more important to be our child's "friend" as opposed to being his or her parent(s), thereby effectively obscuring the authoritative boundary in the child/adult relationship. This is not to say that parents shouldn't be friends with their children, but they should be the kind of friend who sets the standards and direction for positive life progression. This means, first and foremost, being a stabilizing presence of love and support for the child. But it also means being a firm authority figure, and therefore at times, a very unpopular "best friend."

- Passively accepting the extraction of prayer from the public classroom.

- Criminalizing parental discipline and confusing it with what actually constitutes parental abuse.

- Failing to discuss the events of our children's day with them. This prevents parents from remaining engaged and demonstrating ongoing concern for their children's daily activities; a practice that used to be done at the dinner table.

It is vital that we, as members of the Black community, reassert our traditional adult-child perimeters through meaningful and productive engagement, and reclaim our former know-how to effectively produce healthy, well-intentioned offspring. Because presently, many of the "popular" and extensively sanctioned approaches to child rearing seem to result in parents finding themselves often undermined in their authoritative roles and the child becoming the controlling agent and final decision maker in the relational exchange. Though cognitively and emotionally ill-equipped to do so, the child regularly acts as the "demanding" figure in the parent-offspring connection. The parental figure increasingly yields in some form or fashion to the child's commands. Such arrangements are guaranteed to produce insalubrious qualities in one's developing character, as behavioral repetitions soon become entrenched with long lasting effects. The result being, that the once child, now adolescent, soon to be adult, is destined to acquire a dysfunctional sense of entitlement and a narcissistic undergirding that, unless remedied, will augment the chances for expressed traits that reflect a disorder of personality.

Recently, while eating lunch at a McDonald's restaurant, I witnessed a Caucasian child, perhaps five or six years old, mandate to his mother via a temper tantrum that she order him a second ice cream cone, though he had failed to totally consume the one he already had. As I observed the wrangle between mother and child, it became quite obvious that the parent was not the governing presence in their relationship. After the child successfully asserted his power and licked his second cone, he gave his spectators a look of smug accomplishment.

If not properly corrected, what sort of behavior will this child exhibit when he is 10, 15, or 20 years of age?

To achieve a reversal in our present course, we must integrate into our child rearing practices the input, suggestions, and perspectives of our wise elders; those who have reared mostly healthy and productive offspring. I say "mostly" as there is some dysfunction in all of us. Nevertheless, we must adamantly pursue candid dialogue with our elders and achieve meaningful discussion to gain needed insights, and rediscover effective traditional practices of how to suitably address and positively influence the character and behavioral development of our children. We should undertake this at the family and friendship level, collectively within our communities and neighborhoods, and ultimately through open discussions with the greater society (beyond the annual "State of Black America" forum). When considering many of our parental practices and the often-unwise methods of contemporary child-rearing, we are in dire need of altering our course. Too many mothers and fathers often have not experienced or achieved a depth of experiential understanding to maturely guide their thinking and style of responding to their children in the parenting process. The bottom line being, you cannot pass on for others to learn, that which you do not know and understand yourself.

Though trained professionals are very valuable assets in research, diagnosis, and behavioral mediation designs for our children, we cannot rely totally upon those possessing Masters and Ph.D. degrees. Many genuine experts in regard to child rearing never attended an institution of higher learning. In addition, we must recognize the need for implementing more racially specific approaches and behavioral intervention strategies for our youth. The minds of Black children are required to operate in a different manner than their White and "culturally other" counterparts, if they are to function successfully within American society. For example, a Black child's mental processing of media images has to be more discerningly critical than a White child's, since the media consistently promotes multiple negative images of Black people. The White child on the other hand, frequently sees himself portrayed as the situational savior and able to accomplish or achieve practically anything. The Black child must also come to the realization that the degree of behavioral tolerance and disregard for unruliness afforded to others will not often be afforded to him; there remains two distinct judicial systems in America.[35]

To briefly digress, I also venture to say that many of the academically sanctioned "authorities" have never actually reared a Black child, and some others have raised children more emotionally and behaviorally challenged than they are willing to openly admit. My point is that aside from requiring more Black professionals in the field of developmental and child psychology who are willing to promote an Afrocentric model of intervention, we also need to regain the art of nurturing healthy offspring by ensuring that our voices are not drowned out, or our proven traditional practices sullied by those whose publicized behavioral techniques have become "the standard." Some of which, have played an instrumental role in producing the disrespectful, unruly, and "I'm beyond reproach" mindsets of many of today's young.

The present pressures and influences confronting our children necessitate that parents and adults assume an aware, caring, and active role in exposing their minds to prosocial stimuli and healthy thought provoking material. This includes diverting their attention and appetites away from the violent noise of the "gangsta" rapper and the mind trapping lyrics of the hip-hop artist, who provide them with a daily mental diet of anti-social behavior, promiscuous sexual practices, and what often amounts to blatant criminal thinking.

Too many of our young people are not tuned into the voices of knowledgeable, perspicacious thinkers, because in today's Black America these discerning voices are becoming increasingly displaced and supplanted by the attitudes, dialogue, and attractive rhythmic lyrics of trendy peer heroes; media and music stars who along with their producers, are getting rich at the expense of our children. The result being that the voice of Dr. King has been upstaged by the voices of Dr. Dre, Snoop Dogg, 50 cent, Drake, Waka Flocka, Jay Z, and Kanye West. And the voice of Malcolm X has been drowned out by DMX (RIP), Gucci Mane (who was behind bars on a murder charge on the day his LP *Trap House* was released), Lil Wayne, lil Baby, and many others. Today, these and other popularized performers frequently plant dysfunctional mental images and imaginative seeds that undergird the aspirations and behavioral pursuits of our Black youth; scholastically, socially, sexually.

In a study of the influences of sexual lyrics in popular music upon urban youth, Brian Primack, et. al. (2009) states, "In fact, exposure to lyrics describing degrading sex was one of the strongest associations with sexual activity in these models."[36] The study goes on to say: "The relationship between exposure to lyrics describing degrading sex and sexual experiences held equally for both young men and women, which is consistent with the social cognitive theory."[37]

Therefore, the need is not only to address the immediate parental rearing practices that are detrimental to the child's growing character, but to also become more vigilant in regard to the broader social forces that have such devastating effects upon their still developing and vulnerable psyches as well.

Can you imagine, however, the potential shock in our "business as usual" society if we, as mature people of color, began communally harnessing our resources and rejecting that which is counterproductive to our children's emotional and physical existence? Can you imagine the possibilities if we began candidly dialoging on an intimate level with one another and implementing self-preserving grass roots agendas that subscribe to healthier expressions and the prosocial grooming of young people's minds, talents, and perceptions? Can you imagine, the Church, (in mass) stretching beyond its inner-city corner or suburban location, as well as its denominational box, to embrace and connect with the other churches down the block, around the corner and across town, in order to develop and publicize the abilities and positive brilliance of our youth? And here's another thought—how about community churches coming together on a broad scale to create and finance generous scholarship funds to support children on their path to higher education? Instead of building new multi-million-dollar sanctuaries, let's scrap the brick-and-mortar blueprints and use the funds to support the building of young minds.

To carry our remedying efforts a step further, it will become incumbent upon us to determinately strip away the layers of deceit and dishonesty, which has been dispensed on behalf of the Black, the Native American, the Latino, and other minority populations over the years, and begin teaching historical perspectives to our children, as seen through our eyes. Moreover, when considering race and justice in America, we must ask in mass, "Why not teach Critical Race Theory?" The truth must be exposed.

We must seize every opportunity to communicate in fresh and vivid ways, the views acquired from living life in colored flesh, within the context of a white controlled society. That is, communicating valid views from living life on the bottom, views normally given little exposure, unless offered in a style and format that is lucrative and beneficial to media executives.

What would be the impact of these actions? I believe the individuals who currently become wealthy by creating the negative visual, lyrical and literary stimuli for our youth would eventually feel a degree of pressure to modify their practices. I also believe that the mostly unseen personalities who in fact control, condone, and promote the often-skewed depictions of us that we witness in the entertaining and mass media venues would be challenged to correct their maladministration.

* * *

In our literary, musical, and cinematic undertakings, we must consistently validate our perspectives and hold the mirror of reality before ourselves and "majority" America. This however, will be a challenging endeavor, as on the one hand, many of us have difficulty openly and honestly enduring the scrutiny of objective appraisal. We often tend to resist unsettling truth. While on the other hand, that which is positive and sane seems to find less of an audience, as well as promotion, within contemporary media outlets. Nonetheless, we must present a reality that declares just as readily the presence of the Black law-abider as it does the Black law-breaker, the in-tact family as it does the in-crisis family, and the strong and sensible, as it does the weak and senseless.

In regard to "majority" America, honest, open, and balanced accounts of who we are have historically been resisted, as it appears that those who comprise this segment of society collectively preserve their often misinformed ideas of the intellectual, behavioral and moral actualities of nonwhites.[38] Observation would suggest that the "majority" prefer to maintain an uncomplimentary and/or condescending orientation toward us, while existing behind the well-practiced art of self-aggrandizing rhetoric.[39] Hence, and all the more, it is time to stop acquiescing through passivity and self-demeaning behavior to descriptive forgeries and caricatures of our character that does harm to the Black image. Significant numbers of our adult population and youth are not healthy emotionally, behaviorally, or spiritually because they have cognitively embraced invalid images of who they are that were initially promoted by the imaginative processes of those who understand us the least! The consequence being that our evolving sense of Black kinship, our customary Black family practices, and our traditions of faith are being eroded with each successive generation. The very soul-enriched character that was once so sacredly maintained and protected within the Black community, within the Black church, and within the Black heart, is disappearing. And though most of us are aware of this reality on some intuitive level, too many of us stand idly by, too consumed by our own self-interest, or perhaps by a taste of "having arrived," to be engagingly concerned.

A number of years ago, my wife and I took our three children to see the then just released movie starring Queen Latifah and Steve Martin, entitled, "Bringing Down the House." This film had been released under much fanfare, as a "must see" comical "family" motion picture. Indeed, the movie proved to contain a number of laughter producing scenes; however, as my wife and I sat there with our three children, we increasingly became concerned that there were no positive Black men represented by the characters, all were portrayed as partiers, thugs, gamblers, or weed smokers. Yet, the two white male stars were cast as "Attorneys at Law" and one of them, actually won the heart of Black "queen" in the end, who herself was dramatically ghettoized.

This movie prompted an interesting family discussion on the way home, in which we processed the movie's characters, and talked about how we as Black moviegoers, often pay our money to see one sided negative portrayals of us on the cinema screen – Look Black boy child, at that disapproving Black character, this is who you are. Do you see, Black girl child, that Black female actor represents you. But children, do you see the white attorney? Do you see the white romancer? Do you see the white hero, who really deserves the Black queen?

Without the advantage of consistent exposure to the proven wisdom and practices of our cultural elders, it is becoming increasingly evident that we and our children are becoming estranged from our past identity and to one another. Black youth and Black adults are increasingly engrossed in behaviors profoundly different from whom and what our history has projected us to be.

And so, in deceptively simple terms, the Masia warriors of Africa pose a profound question that is particularly relevant for us today: "Kasserian ingera," or "How are the children?" The response that the Masia anticipate hearing when they pose this question to their African brothers is "Sapati ingera," or "All the children are well."[40] How would you reply?

For you and me to honestly answer the question, we have to look at the state of the Black family and household, the state of the Black neighborhood, and of American society across the broad-spectrum. Our children are a reflection of, and a barometer for, existing familial and social dynamics that are in continual process. Our conditions says this current era in which we exist beckons each of us to stand together to impose a better standard. If, however, we choose not to stand together, we ultimately stand to lose our children. That is, both your child and mine.

CHAPTER THREE

Where's Daddy?

Each morning
I go down
to Gansevoort St.
and stand on the docks.
I stare out
at the horizon until it gets up
and comes to embrace
me. I
make believe
it is my father.
This is known
as genealogy.

—Amiri Baraka, "Each Morning"[41]

Our society has consistently advocated the fostering role of the mother. Yet, regrettably, it has historically placed significantly less emphasis on the crucial child-rearing role that fathers play. While the presence of a caring mother cannot be overemphasized, my impression, gained from nearly 30 years of working with delinquent adolescent populations, and supported by study after study, is that an emotionally healthy and engaged father is a critical component to enhancing a child's opportunities for embracing a positive lifestyle and having a prosocial orientation.[42] However, many males fail to develop a sufficient understanding of the significance of their parenting role.

Due to their own protracted exposure to faulty paternal models, many men even with honest intentions, ultimately mimic and embrace a diminished concept of what fatherhood entails. In effect, they negate fulfilling the fatherly role because of learned dysfunctional perspectives consisting of cognitive distortions and a double standard belief system; essentially, failing to become engaged fathers because of deeply entrenched thinking errors.

Parenting education is a first step in helping these males who have an insufficient comprehension of the importance of their nurturing presence in a child's life. In my clinical experience, teaching young men the skills needed to properly engage the parental role can make a considerable positive impact. This is especially true once the young man has opportunity to soberly reflect upon his own childhood and what he gained, or failed to gain, from his own father figure. Still, it takes a good deal of cognitive and emotional maturity for a young or teenage father to authentically want to make the necessary cognitive shifts and put forth the daily effort to effectively parent.

For those whose parental absence stems from a more deeply embedded adherence to misguided belief systems, intervention must take place in a more multifaceted way. For these individuals, meaningful outcomes result from addressing self-images, core ideas related to "manhood", and processing broader social issues.[43] This concentrated endeavor is an uphill climb, because many individuals find it extremely difficult to accept new concepts and alter behaviors once they have entered late adolescence and early adulthood, when their behavioral patterns have become fairly entrenched. Therefore, I believe a fatherhood/motherhood curriculum that explores self-image, identity, and concepts of manhood and womanhood should be introduced to youth even at the elementary grade school level.

Too many young males, imitating negative behaviors of older men, are interested only in the sexual aspect of the male-female relationship and have minimum, if any, long-term intentions of relational commitment with the opposite sex. Within certain spheres of the African-American community, "baby making," or intentionally producing numerous offspring without parental obligation has become a vicious cycle passed down from generation to generation. In reality, it is a contemporary twist to the "Black stud" phenomenon, when, during American slavery a White slave master would use a "Black stud" (if the master didn't assume the task himself) to impregnate his female slaves as the means of augmenting his lucrative pool of free labor.[44] While enslaved, the Black stud was forbidden to officially claim his children because the children belonged to the master. If, by chance, the male slave was afforded the privilege of declaring his offspring, it remained a superficial claim at best, as he stood the very real chance of watching his children being sold to the highest bidder on the auction block, if it became advantageous for the slave owner to sell them. This shuffling and reshuffling of families separated Black men from Black women and their children.

Today, Black males who impregnate females and fail to acknowledge and provide for their children are in effect doing the same thing the slave master did during the times of the slave trade. Through their irresponsible behavior and belief systems, they are creating and perpetuating kin separation. It is a disturbing state of affairs, because too often the present day slave master—in the form of the judicial and penal system, the mental health system, or social services—soon implements its control and regulation over the adults and/or children in some form or fashion and, just as during the days of chattel slavery, the separation, shuffling and reshuffling of family members often begins. These financially stressed and frequently biased institutions can typically offer, at best, only minimal support and opportunity for the full development of the child's talents and potential.

The real life scenario frequently unfolds as follows. A young Black male, who never knew or bonded with the young male who fathered him, in turn, fathers a child. This newly born child is subsequently not granted the opportunity of bonding with his own indifferent father. Soon the child is ill directed by peers or perhaps certain older individuals, as well as by other available deleterious environmental influences. Over time, resentment and anger stemming from situational factors and the sense that he has been parentally cheated begins to surface in the form of delinquent behavior, and the now adolescent child becomes involved with the judicial system.

After spending time under some type of court supervision or confinement, and perchance earning a behavioral, educational, and/ or criminal label or two, the child, without meaningful intervention, graduates to involvement in deeper levels of vice and dysfunction as his thinking becomes more fully entrenched with ruinous belief systems and cognitive distortions. Eventually, he also becomes a parent, and the cycle continues. For far too many, a substantial criminal sentence, chronic emotional frustration, or an early grave is the culminating outcome. These are individuals who years before had been claimed by a "master" because their daddies failed them.

Among the male populations with which I have worked, there are sometimes two or three generations of young men within the same family line whose fathers were under 18 years of age at the time of their conception. There are great grandfathers in their mid to late forties. What is even more alarming is the discovery that, in many cases, each male within the immediate line of descendants has served or is serving time in a juvenile or adult penal system. Sadly, many of these males, who never benefited from the guidance of a stable and mature father figure, have served time in both.

Living one's formative years without the consistent presence of a devoted father becomes a decisive factor in a child's development. When such a child is eventually exposed to a responsible man who attempts to assist him in gaining a foothold in life, the young child or adolescent often has no clue as how to relate. What's more, he has resolved not to trust or respect anyone of the male gender beyond his closest male peer circle of friends; and even then, the trust and respect may be quite superficial. For many, mistrust extends to practically anyone, male or female, who makes the effort to fulfill the role of adult authority.[45]

This phenomenon results in young lives being consumed by dysfunction and rebellion, in addition to the continued creation of unstable male progenitors who lack the knowledge, experience, and commitment to rear their children. What should be a learned progression from boyhood to manhood to fatherhood becomes altogether disrupted, twisted, and negated because of inadequate and ill-equipped teaching models.[46] Instead, the male child is taken care of by mama and now as an adult, believes that women are supposed to take care of him. Hence, he cannot raise his own children because he himself is constantly seeking out a mama.

Just as indefensible is the plight of the Black female child who never experiences a loving father and subsequently develops negative impressions of men in general. Too often, these young girls grow to expect very little in terms of a man's physical and emotional presence, financial support, and healthy nurturance. Once older, and determined to finally encounter "love" from a male, some will look for and find those from the opposite sex who are willing to play "make believe" with them—at least for a short span of time.[47] Like many of their mothers before them, countless numbers of these young Black females find themselves settling for far less than what they deserve from their relationships, as well as from life in general.[48] While experimenting with casual acquaintances and courtships from an early age, they begin to hold their male companions to a very low standard. By the time deeper, sexually involved relationships evolve, the female is thoroughly primed to expect minimum participation from her male partner, and he in turn has acquired the mindset that easily leads him to become an absentee father, if a child is born from their brief union. Again, the crux of the matter is that the male takes full advantage of the low expectations placed upon him from the beginning of his courtship encounters. On the other-hand, if he never had a caring father of his own to model after, he may simply mimic what he is familiar with and reject the fatherhood role regardless of what the female does or does not expect from him.

* * *

Since the end of the Second World War, disjointed families and absent fathers have become growing realities in Black America.[49] Today the Black family is in jeopardy and the projected outcome seems bleak. The initial contributing causes were increased migration to urban areas, economic oppression, and movement toward the nuclear family and away from the traditional extended family system. Currently, it is the Black male's high rate of purposeful absenteeism, incarceration, unemployment, reduced life expectancy, and poor education that is resulting in the Black family being under siege like never before. In combination with these conditions leading to the depleted numbers of suitable and/or available Black men, we must also consider that Black females are seriously exceeding Black males in a number of aforementioned areas, such as life expectancy, the quest for higher education, and the pursuit of professional fields of interest.[50] A resulting consequence, aside from seeking mates from other ethnic populations, is that increasing numbers of Black women may not necessarily be looking for a permanent parental partner, but rather for someone safe and acceptable enough in the short term to help produce a child. Even still, an absent father is an absent father, regardless of the reason for his absence.

All of the above-mentioned elements occur against the backdrop of a noble past, during which time intensely devoted Black male and female relationships were the bedrock of the African-American family experience.[51]

Understand that strength and willful unity in Black male-female partnerships have been normative in our relational encounter. Our history speaks of resilient and dedicated relationships between the sexes, resulting in binding loyalty amid Black men and Black women during times of both triumph and tragedy.[52] Hence, I must ask the question: On a strictly psychological level, what motives are currently contributing to the wane of healthy male/female relationships within the Black community?

In response, I will return to my initial argument and offer that a key determining component is that we, both males and females, have lost our fundamental understanding of and appreciation for our historical identity, which, as a consequence limits our capacity to extend value and significance to one another. Instead, ours is becoming an increasingly self-centered orientation, with our emotional focus becoming severely egocentric. Basically, we are absorbed with ourselves.[53] And though there is a healthy aspect to focusing on the needs of "self," the evidence today, when considering prevalent trends in media, music, and popular culture, is that our self-focused adoration has gotten out of control. We elevate ourselves, while simultaneously regarding those around us as objects to be used for self-serving purposes and gain. Combined with a lack of healthy role models and a diminishing regard for one another, the outlook for enduring Black partnerships and marriages, as well as effective parenting, as alluded to before, begins to look increasingly grim.

Somewhere in the course of our journey, my generation failed to successfully pass on the concepts of valuing others, making personal sacrifices, and respecting the other gender to far too many of those within succeeding age groups. It is revealingly unfortunate that large numbers within our communities fail to absorb and purposely respond to the magnitude of it all.

It disturbs me to hear a Black male referring to the female he once slept with but never really loved with the curt and trendy statement, "That's my no good baby mama." She is now someone he only communicates with out of necessity—if he ever communicates at all. This speaks of an unhealthy self-image and view of the opposite gender, as well as to an ignorance of the dynamics and beauty of male/female intimacy.

I also cringe when I hear, "That's my sorry baby daddy," a prevalent remark uttered by females regarding the male she once was sexually intimate with, has a child by, but has no real commitment and minimal contact. Again, this speaks to an unhealthy self-image and view of the opposite gender, as well as to ignorance about the deeper meanings of "intimate relationship".

In both cases, it is the child who eventually becomes the emotional and behavioral casualty of the parents' immature thinking and actions. Hence, I find myself counseling troubled youth who tell me that his or her father "ain't shit" because he has never been significant or present in the child's life. Others have little respect for their mothers.

I have found that such young people frequently suffer from at least a moderate degree of depression or diminished self-worth, and will often attempt to hide the depths of their emotional pain by acting it out through some form of rebellion or aggression directed toward the nearest convenient person or object. I have also observed that something is often lacking within the child's basic emotional constitution, often evidenced by a detached or disassociated orientation that characterizes their interpersonal relationships; a real predisposition to being dangerously disconnected (see Chapter 1, page 26).

These youth are often hyposensitive in regard to those around them. Unable to bond with others, they find it easy to hurt people emotionally and/or physically. Such children rarely, if ever, experienced consistency in safety, nurturing, and genuine love—the kind of consistency provided by loving parents who have made child rearing their priority. Instead, the children are forced to take a back seat to their parents' ongoing issues, and they become emotionally starved as their developmental needs for nurturance go unmet. Many such children, after extensive exposure to such conditions, simply acclimatize to the dysfunctional dynamics in which they are reared, and eventually, what is unhealthy becomes normal to them. During their early social and interpersonal development, they never have the advantage of experiencing real parental care, or observing and modeling positive relations between the genders. They never obtain the necessary understanding, social skills, and positive emotional support that mature, wiser individuals are supposed to provide. Unfortunately, many of these youth never become enlightened enough in their thinking to abandon the negative behavioral paradigms to which they were exposed. Instead, they replicate in their own lives the model of parents who lived only for themselves, too occupied with their own desires and interest to recognize and respond to the many needs and situational stressors occurring in the lives of their offspring.

* * *

Children, male and female, should be reared in an environment in which a reliably nurturing female parent is in partnership with a reliably nurturing male parent/figure.[54] The child should know what it is to have a positive emotional connection and long-term bond with both a stable mother and a stable father. I believe our children profit most, and our families function best, when cognitively mature and emotionally healthy mothers and fathers are together at the helm of the family unit, acting in the best interests of each other and their progeny. This involves much unselfish love, tested wisdom, and shared sacrifice, because even when the right intentions are present, healthy parenting becomes one heck of a challenge in a society that promotes satisfying self-interest above all else.

We, as Black men, must recognize that being a "real dad" demands that we interact with our children in a way that communicates:

1. I am glad you were born into this world.
2. What you do is important in my eyes.
3. You are definitely cherished and loved.
4. I am here for you.

(This same fundamental communication holds true for real motherhood as well.)

Real fatherhood insists that we are there for our children from day one, that we are active participants in their lives, and that they clearly see our efforts at ensuring that they strive to do what is right and constructive in this world. Only real men can meet the challenge of being real fathers. Today, too many immature and emotionally unhealthy males, who have attained the biological capacity to reproduce, mistakenly assume they have automatically entered into the distinguished realm of manhood simply because they have procreated.

How many of you reading these pages can recall a time when parents assumed the job of child rearing with a degree of attention and seriousness that we frequently do not witness today? If you can recall such times, I am certain you can also remember when children and adolescents interacted with adults in a respectful manner, simply because they were interacting with "adults." It was rare to hear young people cursing or misbehaving while in the presence of "grown folk". Youth responding with "Yes ma'am" and "yes sir" was not passé, and correcting a child who was not your own did not invoke annoyance or anger being directed at you by the child's parent.

While the above speaks to a different era, this chapter cannot be concluded without applauding the present-day Black mothers and fathers who unite, sacrifice, and endeavor to responsibly parent their children. I must also highly commend those who successfully rear emotionally healthy children without the involvement of an equally invested partner. Because my experience and observations suggest that if you discover a youth who is chronically in trouble with authority, one who is intellectually capable but failing in school, or who is involved with gang-banging and violence, chances are you have also discovered a youth who doesn't have either a nurturing mother or nurturing father actively fulfilling the proper role as guardian, guide, and emotional supporter in the home. I must also give credit to youth who, growing up under undesirable circumstances, strive to become socially productive and emotionally healthy, which reveals a resiliency and special determination possessed by certain individuals who achieve remarkable results despite formidable obstacles.[55] Of these latter individuals, I have had the privilege of knowing more than a few.

Allow me to share the case of Jamon[56]

I offer this child as his case is revealing in a number of ways. And yet, he is by no means unique in terms of what many of our young people experience, or in the way they perceive life and others. I counseled this child for a number of years during his confinement in a juvenile correctional facility.

I initially came into contact with Jamon (not his real name) when he was a 13-year-old juvenile offender. He was serving a sentence of 18 to 36 months for property crimes, assaults, and grand larcenies.

Although Jamon was not originally assigned to my caseload, one of the facility's youth supervisors asked me to stop by and "take a look at him". At the time, Jamon was a new arrival who was threatening to smear feces on the walls of his room as soon as his hands were freed from the leather restraints that secured his wrists to his waist due to his combative behavior. The youth supervisor also informed me that Jamon was not responding well to the efforts of his primary therapist, and that he had been "agitated" for most of the morning.

Before visiting Jamon, I tracked down and briefly spoke to the mental health clinician assigned to his case to see if it would be okay if I gave him a visit. The clinician informed me, in an exasperated tone, that this was an extremely emotionally disturbed child and that he, in all likelihood, would prove to be chronically "recalcitrant" and "incorrigible." In short, Jamon was viewed as a hopeless case. After receiving this impression and dismal prognosis from his therapist, I read the child's behavioral and social history. Immediately afterwards, I went to see him.

When I looked through the door's narrow window to his room, I viewed a rather small frame sitting awkwardly on the cement block that served as the platform for a missing thin mattress. Jamon was in wrist restraints and leg shackles to lessen his chances of injuring himself or staff by flailing and kicking about within the close quarters of his cell. In response, he had intentionally urinated on the floor to express his irritation and discomfort. Shirtless, wearing only his boxers, Jamon's face displayed acute annoyance. The scent of urine was unavoidable.

Whenever I viewed such a scene, I always had a fleeting yet keen awareness of rearing three Black children of my own. I believe this recurring experience emerged because, as a committed parent I have become sensitized to the emotional needs of a young child, but also, for the reason that on a cognitive level I possess a well-developed awareness of the societal and prejudiced challenges that many Black children will have to contend with and rise above even when they are well supported and loved. So as I looked at Jamon, I simply saw an individual in a desperate condition, both physically and emotionally, who under the best of circumstances would have a number of odds weighted against him as he struggles to actualize personal relevance in this world. Hence, I did not focus on the words used in his file to label him as "Severely Emotionally Disturbed", or on the impressions offered by his primary therapist ("recalcitrant" and "incorrigible").

I turned to the attending staff member and asked him to unlock the room's door. Stepping over the urine, I walked toward the cement slab where Jamon sat. As I approached, he looked up at me, rolled his eyes, and turned his face toward the wall. Then, in the most hostile tone his 13-year-old voice could muster, he demanded, "Who are you?"

"I'm Mr. Lee," I said. "Somebody told me there's a young man down here that keeps confusing the floor with the toilet, and that this confusion may start including the walls."

"I ain't got nothing confused." His tone remained hostile.

I replied, "Oh, so this is how you do it all the time, even before you were locked up, huh?"

He responded, "Maybe I did, maybe I didn't."

As I had reviewed Jamon's social and behavioral history, my comeback was immediate and straightforward, but also caring.

"I would say that you didn't, but right now you're mad because you don't want to be here, and definitely not like this."

I nodded toward his shackles, as he gave me a quick glance.

"And you're confused about a lot of things in your life, like why you don't have a daddy and why your mama physically abused you. Now, this is how you've decided to show all of us that you're mad at the world and hurting. Look, the way you're choosing to deal with your situation isn't going to get you anywhere. You're locked in a room, half naked, shackled, with smelly pee all over the floor. You can't feel good."

I paused to allow this last comment to sink in.

"How about you and I changing this situation?"

With this, Jamon turned his head and looked at me for more than a brief scan. We maintained eye contact for the first time since I had entered his presence. He could not disguise his pain, and I knew the defensive wall he had erected had been breached. A wise old psychiatrist once told me to look for the place of pain, and then go there and use it as the door to initiate change.

Jamon and I talked for another thirty minutes as I nudged him toward a verbal agreement, in which, in exchange for removing his wrist and ankle restraints, he would be responsible for refraining from peeing on the floor and exhibiting aggression toward the staff members charged with his care. We also agreed to meet again before the end of the day, after he cleaned himself and his floor.

Before leaving, I informed the unit staff that Jamon was ready to clean the room and take a shower. I also noted that I would be recommending his released from the restraints. Although a few staff questioned whether I was taking an unnecessary risk, I was able to convince the administrative powers to approve my recommendation. Upon having his restraints removed, Jamon showered and cleaned his floor without incident. I saw him again that evening and he remained compliant. The following morning, I requested his transfer to my caseload.

Initially, and as expected, improvement in Jamon's behavior was slow. However, after a degree of trust and greater rapport was established, he began to show amazing progress and I continued to work with him over the course of about two and a half years. Within that span of time, he proved (most importantly to himself) to be very intelligent, witty, a good problem solver, and one heck of a chess player. It became very evident that his scores on the intelligence test administered when he was first detained were not indicative of his true cognitive abilities. Jamon was a very clever adolescent; however, he had been labeled as functioning in the "borderline" range of intelligence, which is only a few points above the intellectual disability classification.

It has long been recognized that the results of our most popular standardized intelligence tests often fail to accurately represent the true intellect and cognitive capacities possessed by inner city youth of color. The knowledge and skills-sets that youth like Jamon must use to exist in their formidable environments are not sampled and validated by the tests designers. They are not considered a meaningful measure of one's level of "intellect," although without those skills, children such as Jamon probably would not survive.

Throughout the course of his childhood, Jamon had become quite familiar with negative peer influence, abuse, abandonment, disappointment, and prevarication by the people who comprised his specified world. Because daily existence had been a priority for him, classroom instruction and educational opportunities that did not translate into helping him navigate the immediate dangers and concerns of his reality, failed to hold his attention. What did Jamon care about "American History" when his mother would be absent for the next three or four days getting high in a crack house and there would be no food on the table for dinner?

Within a span of about five months, Jamon had begun to share with me, while frequently in tears, how his mother had often abandoned him and at times beaten him with extension cords or anything else she could get her hands on. He showed me the scars on his back from the beatings, including the peculiar arrow-shaped scars from having been burned with a hot cloths iron.

Jamon showed me his emotional scars as well. He shared with me how he had never known his biological father and eventually, I gained enough of his confidence to discover how an older adult male had also physically abused him. In time, he painted a picture for me of what he really thought, at his young age, of the world in which he lived—a world in which a child like him, with great potential and talent rarely gains adequate support and opportunity to develop, much less excel, in his abilities; a world in which a damaged and confused child is often considered "recalcitrant" and "incorrigible" because, for him, continuance of life is the name of the game and trusting others only guarantees more pain and betrayal, if not death.

Following my work with Jamon, he was accepted into a group home of excellent reputation. However, as the time approached for his release from confinement, his behavior regressed in the form of becoming oppositional toward staff members. He earned institutional sanctions which threatened to delay his release. It was clear to me that this acting-out stemmed from his anxiety related to being separated from the guidance, structure, and support that he had never before experienced.[57] Ultimately, his release was deferred for about three months, while we worked through his anxieties and fears about facing new and old hurdles that awaited him once he transitioned back into free society.

I will long remember our final session together, the day before he entered his group home. Jamon stared at me with a slight grin, which I had come to recognize as an indication of his attempts to form conclusions. After a brief pause, he stated with conviction, "You're a Muslim."

We had discussed religion before, as this had proven to be one of his many topics of interest, and he knew my confession of faith, but I decided to entertain his comment to see where he was going with it.

I responded, "No, I am a Christian."

Jamon's grin became more pronounced and he repeated with conviction: "You're a Muslim!"

I replied, "No, you know I profess Christianity, but what makes you say that?"

His answer struck me like a sucker punch out of nowhere. With great sincerity, without grinning or breaking eye contact, Jamon said: "Because the Christian men I know don't talk to you straight-up the way you do. Only Muslim men do."

I could only look at him, as he went on to state that in his neighborhood "Christian people" hadn't said much of anything to him that he could recall. All he really associated with Christians was our dressing well on Sunday mornings and driving past kids like him on the way to church. (A frequent reality I now refer to as "the Christian drive-by," because it can have harmful consequences for innocent children, just like the drive-bys of those who fire loaded weapons, except the result may be long enduring or permanent emotional scars as opposed to physical ones).

Jamon's comment forced me to step back and take a long, serious look at myself and the Christian community. I must admit, the picture I saw revealed that many of us only want a "feel good" religion. Perhaps, because of the pain and uncertainty in our personal lives, we often hesitate to step into the lives of others, including our children's (I say "our children's" in the broad sense). Too often we will turn away from places that require us to display transparency and to be profoundly real in our concern and love—places where it is essential to maintain candidness, with a mindset of determination and faith, while viewing ours and other's situation within the given context exactly as it is.[58]

As I continued to reflect upon the depth of what Jamon had said in that final session, it made me want to scream out for real men and fathers, for real women and mothers, to step up to the plate in our inner cities and suburban neighborhoods, indeed in all communities, to purposely create conditions that better ensure the survival and achievement of the young. Our nurturing presence and healthy multigenerational engagement is vital for the wellbeing of our youth and communities.

In the final analysis, I believe I benefited more from that final session with Jamon than he did from me, because his comments have made me acutely aware that young boys, girls, and teenagers are watching us with a critical eye; we who are older and supposedly mature; we who profess a faith that stands upon love and sacrifice. Indeed, I carry this awareness in my profession, in my home and neighborhood, as well as in the broader society.

I want to thank all of the "Jamons" who have allowed me to become a part of their worlds, because for sure, they have become a part of mine.

* * *

With the increased popularity of same sex relationships, along with statistics showing that a high percentage of today's marriages end in divorce, the concept of "family" being comprised of two committed opposite sex adults is indisputably fading. We are gradually losing the conventional family unit. Remember that once popular arrangement involving a devoted male husband, a devoted female wife, and their children?

Of course, I am aware that there are many who argue that single and same sex partnerships can provide all that an opposite sex marriage/partnership can offer. And I hear your arguments, as there are, and will continue to be, success stories. However, I respectfully propose that a single parent or same sex partner relationship cannot provide the same intuitive emotional, physical, and cognitive balance that a healthy opposite sex partnership provides. The sexes are different, naturally. We (men and women) often think and reason differently, we often prioritize as well as spend our past time differently, we play differently, we communicate differently, for sure, we are different beyond our physical makeup. Yet, it is the healthy expression of these differences that provides balance and enriches the effectiveness of rearing emotionally healthy offspring.

My personal experience in treating the many mental health issues occurring within the adolescent psyche suggests that children want to experience this balance. Youth appear to have an inborn desire for involved mothers and fathers.

So again, can a single parent successfully rear a child? Though often very challenging, the answer is yes. Can same sex partners successfully rear a child? Longitudinal studies appear limited, but many within the research community offer that indeed they can. Nevertheless, based on the fundamental co-sexual arrangement naturally employed for our very existence, which I believe, was divinely designed, I posit that children not only crave, but are innately created to developmentally benefit from a healthy parental union between a man and a woman. The necessary contribution of the male and female in the phenomenon of human replication extends far beyond the required biological component of egg and sperm. Needless to say, current observation often suggests that we fail to acknowledge and recognize the extent of this vital male-female conjoining effort. In considering the issue of parenthood, our children are afforded a disservice when we actively dismiss or minimize the many positive behavioral and character influences that nourishing opposite gender members provide along the full spectrum of one's personality development.

Today's drift toward forfeiting the most basic and longstanding social institution—the traditional family—is, in my opinion, only augmenting the chances that our young will increasingly face arduous adolescent and adulthood issues related to becoming emotionally secure, with dismaying outcomes in regard to their developing temperaments and long-term behavior.

* * *

As a Black child growing up in an urban community, my appreciation for having been exposed to the male/female parental equilibrium cannot be overstated. There was a sense of completion within the relational dynamics of the family unit that gave me a sense of ease and acceptance at home that was unparalleled in other settings. Home was always my "base." It was the place of safety, and there was a comforting attraction to being "at home." And though at the age of seventeen I ventured off to further my education, the gratification of being reared by both parents, at home, has only grown stronger throughout the years.

It was in the home that my parents taught and reinforced through the use of positive and negative consequences, the difference between "right" and "wrong" behavior. It was there that my socio-cognitive development and moral conscience gained its footing. Indeed, how my mother and father responded to and regarded various events and activities occurring in my immediate and broader environment substantially influenced my thinking. And, of course, there were significant others who had a profound influence upon me as well, such as extended family members and certain others in the community. Together with my parents, they comprised the system that provided my ethical and behavioral foundation, my primary roots.

This occurred in the not so distant past, when civil rights, Black pride, church attendance, and a common vision for both community and self-improvement was prominent; when principled standards were widely shared; when most parents did not jump to the defense of their young when a neighbor, teacher, friend, or even a stranger chastised them for misbehaving. Instead, adults took into account feedback from other adults and responded to their children accordingly. It was the not so distant era when being educated was widely sought after, promoted and smiled upon. To achieve scholastically at any grade level was highly respected within the adult community and by most of one's school aged peers.

Very early during my elementary school experience, I began to realize that my parents expected me to continue my education beyond high school, though neither of them had attended college. My father never earned an abundance of money; however, he began purchasing U.S. savings bonds before I was born. His foresight and planning allowed the college dream to become a reality for his children. Early awareness of my responsibility to myself and my family, along with a very positive regard for what it meant to be a Black person, provided me with the motivation to pursue the higher education that my parents envisioned.[59] This same sense of responsibility also motivated me to successfully navigate the urban environment whenever challenges and obstacles arose—the same challenges and obstacles that continue to derail the lives of young Black males and females today, whose directional focus is misguided or unsteady.

At a young age, I recognized that there was a moral and behavioral standard I needed to adopt in order to obtain positive reinforcement and to avoid punishment. Whenever my parents discovered that I had initiated or participated in activities of which they disapproved, there were always penalties, the severity of which was determined by the severity of the misdeed. These repercussions ranged from a simple glaring look that put you on notice, to stern lectures, to timeouts (standing in a corner facing the wall), to spankings. And mom preferred switches for the latter, which my sister and I had to collect from a bush that grew in the yard beside our home. At the time, I swore that some sadistic individual had planted that bush solely for the purpose of providing switches for my mother. Nevertheless, as my sister and I (mostly I) collected our switches, we were never abused, and we both knew in the balance of things, that we were very much cherished and loved. No spanking ever occurred without a sober explanation of the reason for the punishment and then a verbalized statement or two of what was expected behaviorally in the future. My last spanking occurred when I was 9 years old, by then, I realized that there was an uncompromised standard ever before me, and I was afterwards quite responsive to verbal correction.

When I was about eight years old, I recall my father spanking me after I blatantly disobeyed him in an attempt to impress an older cousin. After apprising me of my misdeed, I recall dismissing the statement dad made before rendering the punishment: "Son, this is going to hurt me more than it hurts you." My unvoiced thought was, "yeah right!"

Once the spanking was over, I immediately heard sniffling in addition to my own. I turned to see tears in my father's eyes. At the time it was quite perplexing; however, after becoming a man with my own children, I clearly understood.

Though I was far from a perfect child, there were boundaries I learned not to cross. I can recall making excuses to my adolescent friends, telling them I had to go home, when their activities strayed from what my mother and father would have approved. Deep down, having my parents' good opinion of me meant more than gaining the temporary approval of my peers.

By the time I had grown beyond the age of spankings, my relationship with my parents had developed into a deep-seated respect. It was this respect that motivated me to continue to manage my behavior in later years, though, in all honesty, I went through a period of behavioral callousness while in college. But even then, I had strong convictions about personal responsibility and behavioral choices. Consequently, whenever I crossed the line into inappropriate activity, I experienced a healthy guilt response—healthy, because it motivated me to eventually correct my misbehavior.

It was at home that I also gained a high level of respect for the opposite sex. The respect I developed for my mother translated into a high level of respect for my sister, which in time translated into respect for females in general. Coming up, I never heard females being referred to as "hoes" or "bitches" by my mother or father. Those words were simply never used in our home.

My parents, together with extended family members and an alert and caring community (our little inner city "village"), committed themselves to the job of raising, correcting, and protecting the "kids." Because of this, I grew up without the need for the intervening efforts of a probation officer, a social worker, a paid mentor, or an in-home counselor. I also grew up without a police record or experiencing juvenile incarceration. Most of the grown-ups around my peers and me were diligent in rearing us, but for me, the most essential modeling and nurturance came from my mother and father.

As a child, I watched how my father earned the respect of both males and females, because he respected them. I watched him work and at times come home exhausted, but get up the following morning and again go to work. I watched him as he was both stern and tender with my sister and me. I watched, as he was always there for family and how he very highly esteemed our mother. There was something deep within me that identified with him because early on, I recognized the physical likeness between us. And I watched my mother. I saw how she carried herself with dignity and how she authentically cared for her family and others. I saw her faith. I saw in what ways she was sensitive. I saw her strength. And though profound respect, admiration and love were present for my mother, I knew that in some very obvious ways, our likeness was limited. But it was okay, because there was a healthy male in the house who's likeness I shared. All things considered, I witnessed the balance within my parent's relationship—man and woman together contributing to the parental responsibility of rearing my sister, me, and eventually, one of my female cousins. The full impact of what they did and sacrificed for us as children did not become meaningful to me in a palpable way, until while attending graduate school and being hired as a counselor, I walked into a medium security prison, my first day on the job, and encountered two childhood friends in prison garb.

For them, the degree of dysfunction in their immediate families outweighed the various stabilizing influences available within the neighborhood and community. One friend had family members who were no strangers to criminal courtroom proceedings, and a physically volatile father. The other did not have a father figure in the home. His mother, though she tried hard to raise him, was in many ways an enabler. While her son persisted in testing behavioral limits, she excused much of his wayward behavior and defended many of his offensive antics. Looking back, I can easily recall incidents that revealed the path these two individuals were on, initially due to no fault of their own.

Each began earning failing grades in elementary school. Rebellion against adult authority soon followed. Unsurprisingly, as teens, they were officially labeled with behavioral indicators and cognitive deficits. These labels invoked a vigilantly cautious response from various others, and they were ultimately treated differently from the rest of us in school and by some within the community. In return, these two individuals gravitated toward delinquent opportunities often inspired by criminally minded older peers who took them under their wings. Because they could not adequately articulate it at the time, they expressed their unmet emotional needs and desire for parental structure and love through misbehavior, poor school performance, and seeking others who would validate them.

Many years later, my childhood friends, now young men, greeted me as inmates in a prison yard on the first day of my employment as a counselor. It was a bittersweet reunion, and my escort thought I was crazy, as my old friends and I instinctively gave each other "dap" and a hug. I was in route to my office, they to their cellblock. As we stood on the prison yard, they told me about their charges and the amount of time they had to serve. When my turn came to briefly catch them up on some of the details my life, it felt odd. We had come from the same community, had run and played together as children, had hung out as adolescents and yet, had traveled down very different paths. As we exchanged stories, countless amusing childhood and teenage memories flashed through my mind. It was good speaking to my old friends, though painful to see guard towers and razor wire serving as the backdrop to our conversation.

After that day's encounter, we had infrequent direct contact. Though they often gave me approving nods from a distance that said, "Do your thing, brother", they rarely approached me out of respect for the very different reasons we were behind the wire. Appearing to be too friendly with an inmate could prove to be problematic for all involved. We were together, but living in different worlds; worlds that clearly had their genesis in how our parents reared us.

PART II

The Calibration: Let's Talk

I find myself at a place in life where my experiences and perspectives compel me to offer my impressions for others to consider. Perhaps this is because many of the opinionated voices that resonates the loudest in mainstream media often fail to reflect my thoughts, appraisals, and points of view. As well, human conditions and patterns of interpersonal exchange which I witness at times create the impulse in me to speak out even when perhaps the only impact will be my own emotional venting.

As we move into the second part of this text, I wish to explore a few issues that repeatedly appear front and center in the news today. They include, educating our children, political ideologies, and a third topic that calls for exploration in a very candid fashion, that is, racist thinking and behavior (intentional or otherwise). Education, the machinery of politics, and race designation all play their part in shaping our lives.

* * *

Certainly, this section will spark controversy as it evokes various opinionated responses depending upon one's personal experiences within his or her specified world. So, once again, I urge you to soberly reflect and comment upon the content. Let's commence our dialogue.

CHAPTER FOUR

Education

Fitting the Pieces of the Puzzle

Considering the downright disproportionate number of Black youth, especially males, who annually fail to earn a high school diploma, it should concern us all that the methodology of public education basically remains unchanged year after year. The *2010 Schott 50 State Report on Black Males and Education* reported that the 2007-2008 national graduation rates for Black males was a dismal 47%.[60] Forty seven percent! With an increase to only 59 percent by 2019. This is a continuing crisis, yet, one that is solvable.

TiAja Ellis (2010) discusses the distressing Black male dropout percentage in an article entitled "Are Black Male High School Drop-Out Rates Hurting America?"[61] Ellis examines the social and economic consequences of failing to gain an education, not only for the uneducated individual, but also in terms of the detrimental effects suffered by society as a whole.[62] Ellis cites Peter D. Hart & Associates 2006 national high school report, *The Silent Epidemic*, which describes the social impact as follows: "Our communities and nation lose productive workers and incur higher costs associated with increased incarceration, health care, and social services."[63]

Within the learning environment, our youth seek out that which provides them with a sense of cognitive stimulation, self-worth, and pride; educators and school administrators are very aware of this. If little can be found within the school venue and sanctioned curriculum to satisfy the aforesaid children's combination of needs, you can be sure that they will use their creative energy to produce their own cherished sense of personal prominence, heightened self-esteem, "knowledge" to master, and even meaningful rites-of-passages to pursue. As well, they will identify their own relevant peer instructors. Unfortunately, when the desire for cognitive stimulation, self-worth, and pride isn't supervised under the guidance of a knowledgeable, concerned and invested adult, youth will often seek to fulfill those wants through negative behavior. This partially explains the conundrum of why gangs have become so pervasive in so many schools and neighborhoods. Where home, community, and the educational system fail them, gangs pick up the slack and provide impressionable young people with a sense of belonging, acceptance, "special knowledge," and tutors.

I've come across adolescents who have failed practically every classroom subject offered, yet demonstrate the ability to accurately learn and memorize a gang's rituals, symbols, codes, and complex language. Turned off by public education and often feeling as though there is no authentic connectedness with their educators, the child or adolescent discovers cognitive stimulation and personal significance by other means.

From my perspective, one of the most disquieting aspects of this dilemma is that the problem persists, though many educational programs have proven to succeed in appealing to the mental energy of the Black child. In such cases, there is a significant increase in the child's academic interest and achievement far above the national norm, as in the model set forth by Providence St. Mel School in Chicago, Illinois.[64] St. Mel has boosted a 100% college acceptance rate for its graduating seniors every year since 1978.[65] And though St. Mel is a private institution, I question what prevents its duplication in the public sector, since it is manifestly evident that when the right approach is taken, the right outcome is achieved. Indeed, the educational crisis is solvable. So what stands in the way? And who should be leading the charge for change?

I propose that it is our politicians and school administrators who regularly serve as inoperative catalyst for change. Their often-restricted focus and practices play a major part as to why our learning environments are what they are—places of failure for far too many Black children. In response to them, I suggest that creative oriented principals, teachers, parents and communities pick up the cause and demand major change. Successful programs are led by those who think outside the box.

With the perennial pedagogical predicaments affecting the degree and quality of learning occurring throughout our public educational systems, we must point out and question any politician who considers cutting funding for public schools as a worthwhile pursuit for budget balancing. As well, school boards that appear to work against generating innovative thinking and increased pay for deserving teachers, along with administrators who lack effective transformational vision or who hinder career advancement for worthy educators must be pointed out and candidly questioned. On a more immediate level, teachers who are unable to create stimulating on-site instructional environments to promote learning excellence, should be held accountable and replaced. Our schools require leaders and instructors with foresight, as well as organizational and managerial skills that spawn excitement, and which lures all involved to buy into the program envisioned. And of greatest importance, our youth must experience motivational energy by gaining a deeper understanding of the significance of intellectual enlightenment. Thus, it is essential that they experience frequent exposure to those deserving to be modeled after academically. As well, our children require confirmatory support from concerned teaching staff and involved parents. In short, they must have enhanced opportunity to adopt personally relevant reasons to respond to their learning opportunities in a positive fashion. But there is more.

It is critical that instructors do not stereotype Black youth or embrace a "majority" American mentality in regard to Black talent and potential; i.e., exceptional performance anticipated on the sport's field of play, but not within the academic fields of science, mathematics and literature. To do so only increases the chance that approaches to instruction and developmental interventions will be ineffective or provide less impact than needed for achievement (the evidence of which we so clearly see today). When lesson plans and teaching styles become unsuccessful, the student soon harbors little respect for the teacher, and the teacher, in turn, has ample opportunity to encounter feelings of disapproval and frustration toward the student. Perhaps this is a contributing factor as to why a disproportionate number of Black children (Black males in particular) start forming negative impressions of their classroom instructors and begin persistently underachieving by the fourth grade; a culturally specific phenomenon known as "the fourth-grade syndrome."[66] In his book entitled, *Countering The Conspiracy To Destroy Black Boys* (1980), Jawanza Kunjufu's data continues to hold relevance today. Kunjufu points out that Black students enter first grade with positive feelings about themselves and their schools, but by the second grade many have already started developing negative feelings about their teachers and the learning environment, leading to feelings of cynicism by the fourth grade.[67] Consequently, by the time these students enter the fifth grade, negative attitudes toward teachers and education have already been formed, often with academically disastrous consequences.

Teachers, regardless of race, who come from circles of existence far removed from the worlds of many of our youth may be at a disadvantage, at a core psychological level, in terms of effectively communicating with, and behaviorally guiding those who are Black and culturally different in their classrooms. The result being, educators who have the right intentions may have difficulty authentically connecting with the Black child in a manner that says to him "you are respected and valued." For some, this break down may result from an ethnocentric judgmental orientation steeped in existent underlying unexamined biases, and for others, it may simply stem from a lack of understanding the dynamics at work within the child's subculture, or social economic realities. Considering the aforementioned, the effort to address our children's educational needs must extend beyond the formal classroom environment in very real ways.

* * *

Too many Black youth fail to learn their weekly math lessons and master proper sentence structure, yet, on cue, can repeat verbatim the rhythmic lyrics of popular songs and raps. Too many dismiss bringing their assignments home to study, yet are given liberty to watch their favorite nightly cartoons or television programs. Large numbers of Black youth reject the idea of reading a book, but seize every opportunity to listen to the latest music on their multimedia devices. Many forego spending significant time studying on weekends, but have plenty of time to hang out in the streets, show up at the mall or go to the movies. Consequently, in all fairness there is an imbalanced share of responsibility being placed on public school teachers for a child's academic progress or lack there-of.

At a very early age, well before preschool, mothers and fathers need to begin providing structured, mind-enriching activities, along with consistent and beneficial child rearing and teaching practices for their children. Or, if necessary, these endeavors must be implemented by mama or daddy alone, as increasingly, there is only one parent available in the home.

It is of utmost importance that parents assume more accountability and responsibility for supporting their children's educational experience when they are outside the classroom. At the same time, parents must tirelessly press for relevant mind enriching school curriculums and programming such as being implemented at Providence St. Mel, as previously mentioned, in Chicago.

CHAPTER FIVE

Racism

My father once told a story about how he and other family members, including an infant, were traveling through the South by car one summer during the 1950's. Upon stopping at a gas station to refresh themselves, tired and thirsty, they had no choice but to drink from a greasy hose that was used to put water into car batteries and radiators. Why? The only available water fountain was clearly marked, "Whites only."

Racism in practice, regardless of the degree, time, or form, is always ugly.

* * *

There is little that directly affects the operational dynamics of American society so much, and yet, remains so casually dismissed and minimized as much, as racism. It is a multi-layered, multifaceted, socially engrained complication that arises in economics, politics, and religion. And although wanton racism provoked both a bloody civil war and an overdue civil rights movement on American soil, America has thus far failed to fully confront and come to grips with its racist past or present reality. For the most part, racism is a common, daily practice that receives little attention until some revealing event or blatant remark spills over into the public arena and places it at the forefront of mainstream media reporting. At least until the next news worthy occurrence pushes it once more aside, and again, allows countless individuals to refute its presence.

On average, Caucasians view racism as being much less of a problem and less widespread as compared with how Blacks typically perceive it.[68] Meanwhile, practically everyone is affected or involved in some way. Some observers do acknowledge the continued existence of racism, but most carry on in regards to it, in a Pollyannaish fashion. Only a few actually attempt to constructively deal with its effects. Though even for this group, often their efforts appear more superficial than sincere.[69]

Before continuing, I must offer that I view racism as a very intentional practice carried out by representatives of the ruling race, or race in power, directed towards representatives of another race that is without, or with significantly less power. This intentional practice is scientific, calculated, and intended to be degrading, oppressive, unjust, and unfair, towards those to whom it is directed, in order to damage their self-esteem, self-image, and life progression, as to affect their immediate and/or long-range quality of existence. Those within the ruling race preserve this practice through their advantage of power, which is accomplished by creating, promoting, and sanctioning interpersonal traditions, official legislation, and methods of "conducting business".

In practice, racism occurs at two levels:

(1) Those belonging to the power race who are directly involved in creating, promoting, and sanctioning

harmful real life practices directed towards another race.

(2) Those belonging to the power race, involved in willingly following, implementing, and when need be, improvising, as regarding created, promoted and sanctioned harmful real life practices directed towards another race.

In contemporary society, the most potent and successful practitioners of this demeaning way of viewing and treating those who are culturally different, do not wear hooded sheets or attend cross-burning ceremonies under the cover of darkness in some farmer's field. Instead, today's racists often serve as elected government officials, own businesses, and pride themselves on wearing starched shirts, suits, and fashionable neckties. Today's racists are found occupying important occupational posts, and he or she is sure to use politically correct speech when operating outside the security of their cliques. Though this has dramatically changed following the presidency of Donald Trump, as his presence on the scene fanned the smoldering embers of racism within American society reflective of a time more akin to the pre-civil rights era. Prior to his time in the oval office, the more immediate racist code of conduct was more about stealth and illusion, encompassing the skill of appearing to be something that he or she was not (racially fair). And though many modern racist still cleverly mask their intentions and motives, humans do eventually err, and by erring, reveal what's beneath the outward facade.

During his 2006 re-election campaign, Virginia Senator George Allen, in a moment of campaign excitement while at an outdoor rally, referred to a young, dark complexioned male (who was of Indian origin) as a "macaca."[70] The term is a derogatory racial slur, meaning either "monkey" or "African migrant." [71] Had someone not videotaped the comment on a cell phone and made it available to the news media, the Senator (and former Virginia Governor) would have likely gotten away with what I am certain he had gotten away with for years. But it proved to be a highly publicized slip of the tongue which cost him his bid for re-election. At the time, it was also highly suspected that "Senator Allen" had his sights on making an eventual run for the White House. And how about on August 01, 2011 Congressman Doug Lamborn (R-Colorado) referred to President Obama as a "tar baby."[72] Curiously, this name calling was not highly reported in major media outlets.

Of late, there have been politicians, very well-paid radio personalities, and now a former President whose remarks or persistent publically focused attention reveals the presence of an orientation that is racially narrow-minded and indicative of pure racist thinking.[73] Every one of the innocent Central Park 5, would have been executed if Trump would have had his way.

One plausible explanation for this appears to be that within some well-preserved mental construct of many White Americans, is the notion that they continue to own us; perhaps related to an obsession to dominate. Whatever the underlying reason, the consequence is that it really exposes one's visceral orientation. This is what makes the likes of a Clarence Thomas, or a Herman Cain so attractive to this faction. Such individuals are trusted to further a certain cause because they are perceived as being owned. Nothing can be more revealing in this regard than the statement made by political conservative Ann Coulter on October 31, 2011 while speaking with Sean Hannity on his Fox News program. When referring to Black Republicans vs. Black Democrats, Ann commented, "Our Blacks are so much better than their Blacks."[74] A very illuminating remark! Aside from saying that her/their Blacks, in her thinking, unreservedly cooperate to champion their agenda, she implied ownership of all of us.

Jack David of the University of Connecticut, who has researched racism for 30 years, suggests that 80% of White Americans "have racist feelings they may not even recognize."[75] The effects of this "unrecognized" racism can be detected from courtrooms to boardrooms, from politicians to policemen, from fair housing to fair education, from media coverage to medical coverage, and from equal pay to equal opportunity. For the latter example, the wealth gap between Black and White America is extremely enlightening.[76] In fact, racist feelings, recognized or unrecognized, play a prominent role in how we approach and treat each other in our simple everyday encounters. For those who take note, this truth easily becomes apparent. Aside from the ownership orientation, the racial attitude frequently directed towards us who are Black, in Black and White social engagements outside of clearly structured settings, often takes the form of what I refer to as "Blackfolkophobia," a phenomenon based upon deep-seated stereotyping. Allow me to share an example.

On a summer afternoon, after throwing a football with my two teenage sons, I invited them out for ice cream at a local parlor a few miles from our suburban community. When we arrived, people were standing outdoors in two lines waiting to be served, so my sons and I moved behind those in the shorter line.

A few moments after the last couple in front of us had collected their order and departed, my younger son whispered, "Dad, do you notice anything?"

My sons and I happened to be the only Black people there, and looking around, I noticed that the three of us stood alone in our line. Mind you, more customers were continuing to arrive, so that at least eight or nine individuals occupied the line next to us. As I stepped toward the counter to place our order, I couldn't decide if what I was witnessing from the other patrons was merely coincidental or an indication of something else. For the adroit observer, the scene would have provided a snapshot of a racial divide that, in times past, spurred marches and boycotts.

I must admit that the situation was somewhat amusing. The White customers not only chose to stand in a longer line in the afternoon sun, but they also kept glancing in our direction. Some permitted themselves longer gazes, as if we were three Black male enigmas requiring guarded study. While we waited for our ice cream, I entertained myself by imagining the thoughts of those who examined us.

"Why aren't they sporting hip-hop attire?" "

How come they aren't speaking Ebonics?"

"The baldheaded one looks like a criminal."

"Could they be his sons? No, can't be. Something's fishy!"

Since no one dared move from the longer line to our shorter one, I finally came to the conclusion that our perplexed onlookers were convinced we were packing pistols with the intent of robbing our server and making a hasty escape, no doubt, leaving trails of melting ice cream in our wake. Whatever their actual thinking was, no one ventured to stand behind us while we placed our order. Far too risky I suppose.

During and following my brief self-entertainment, I also experienced a wave of annoyance. This feeling, I am sure, was more for my sons than for myself, because I realized they were confronting the sensation that many Black males experience when in the presence of unfamiliar Whites—suspiciously watched and/or made to feel uninvited and/or uncomfortably different. I couldn't help but reflect upon the stories told by older Blacks of the deliberate conditions of public separation with which they had to contend in years past. Indeed, while standing there, I could not help but consider the words: "judged not by the color of your skin, but by the content of your character." Looking at my two Black sons, I also concluded that the uncertainty and fear often induced by crowd psychology, stereotypes, and media myths regarding the Black male remains an indisputable part of our society. The separation of the races into two distinct color lines at an ice cream parlor suggested to me, once again, that racial progress hasn't really progressed as far as some choose to think.

After paying the bill and exiting the parking lot, I bit into my chocolate fudge ice cream cone and glanced in the rearview mirror. I wasn't surprised. The two lines were now fairly evenly occupied.

* * *

On October 21, 2010, National Public Radio (NPR) news analyst Juan Williams, a Black man, offered comment regarding Muslims that sounded disquietingly similar to those directed toward Black men for decades. While speaking on the NPR News Channel, in reference to flying on commercial airliners, Mr. Williams stated, "If I see people who are in Muslim garb and I think, you know, they are identifying themselves first and foremost as Muslims, I get worried. I get nervous." [77] Consequently, NPR fired Mr. Williams, but Fox News quickly increased his commentary role and the monetary contract he held with them.[78]

When I heard Williams' comments, my initial thought was, "This guy is suffering from the illusion of inclusion," or a mental orientation that is more in line with the collective White psyche than with his own people of color. His opinionated remarks sounded out of place coming out of the mouth of a Black American, as they reflected more of a European, paranoid, xenophobic thought process regarding a cultural other.

Perchance it is difficult for Mr. Williams to fathom this, but if he were to put on sunglasses and a Sean John sweat suit, and then step onto a small crowded public elevator occupied by four or five average White folk who couldn't sufficiently space themselves apart from him, they would probably get a bit "nervous"; feel a little uneasy. Yes, his perception of inclusion is at the very core, only an illusion.

* * *

I found it a remarkable incongruity to have initially written this chapter when a Black man, whose father was a

Muslim, was serving in the highest elected office our nation has to offer. But then again, our society has always provided opportunity for extreme incongruities, i.e., "... we hold these truths to be self-evident, that all men are created equal ..." "Created"? "Equal"?

I believe the main reason so much vehemence and vilification was directed toward a Black President who actually won by popular vote (no Supreme Court intervention was needed to get him into office[79]) is because those within the circles from which the derisive comments develop believe the following, "No Black man in America is supposed to be serving in the political office of United States President!" If we are to allow ourselves to be blatantly honest, we must conclude that much of the resistance to our 44th President was not as much about political views, opinions, and governing principals or policy, as it was about his race. Mr. Obama was at times the most politically capitulating president that I can personally recall. He sincerely seemed to desire to govern from a locus of maturity that rose above the bad feelings of numerous groups concerning his race. Even still, for many individuals, the undeniable fact that he is a Black man (as determined by America's own rules regarding racial designation, though this is changing, as "bi-racial" is becoming increasingly popular) could not be stomached. The degree of opposition in Washington by certain Senators and Congressmen to practically everything that was Obama lead or initiated speaks to something very personal. Based on their tenacious political activities in response to him, one must conclude that there are definitely those within the D.C. beltway that share the attitude represented by the White man who leaned out his vehicle's window and yelled, "F—k

Obama!" as he drove past my family and me as we sat in traffic. At the time, I had an "Obama for President" sticker displayed in the back window of my car. Even still, we must appreciate the fact that Mr. Obama would not have gained the White House without the vote of those representing the differing racial factions in this country, especially that of those who are White.

As an aside, I found it intriguing, that it made the national news when President Obama designated himself as "Black" on the 2010 census? [80] The prevailing day's headlines and news coverage offered something along the lines of "Obama Checks Black." [81] Up until that point, many within the American "majority" and news media seemed bent on subtly (and at times not so subtly) promoting the "mixed race" designation; an argument that again gained some footing with the arrival of Herman Cain upon the political scene. The idea being that because there is White ancestry in Obama's family line, he's not really Black but instead "Bi-racial", Herman Cain is Black. Amazing! There are White ancestors somewhere in the family lines of most of us. Not to mention Indian, Asian, and whoever else was attracted to the beauty of Blackness.

* * *

An interesting psychological paradox occurred when many of Mr. Obama's most ardent critics, in spite of themselves, were sincerely obliged to give him a brief period of reprieve, and credit, while they relished in the well-executed plan that resulted in the killing of Osama Bin-Laden. But this period or reprieve was indeed quite brief, and many spontaneously felt compelled to give a share of Obama's earned acclaim to George Bush Jr. After all, they argued, wasn't it Bush Jr. who initiated the search for Bin-Laden in the first place? Boy! And within a few days, it was back to business as usual. Blame for the debt crisis, unemployment, and a poor economy resumed its previous place on Obama's shoulders. With the subsequent over throw of Libya there was barely a mention of how President Obama's politics influenced the process.[82] If either of the aforementioned events would have occurred during his predecessor's watch, we would still be hearing of the extraordinary political savoir faire exercised on behalf of the President to complete undertakings that further secured the safety of America. But neither event took place under the watch of George Bush. Though a number of very important events did, so personally, I continue to await the ardent and repeated argument that "Wasn't it Mr. Bush Jr. that spent every available cent and more of the surplus left in the national budget by President Bill Clinton. And didn't Mr. Bush support the idea that increased wealth for the wealthy is somehow beneficial for the economy and for the rest of us. Not to mention his use of extremely flawed intelligence that set this nation on the course of war that continued for 20 years.

* * *

Observation would suggest that Black men produce a special anxiety within the psyches of many, if not most of White Americans. This is especially true for Black men who "identify themselves first and foremost as Black," while appearing to be "out of place" in their socioeconomic status, residential location, career advancement, willingness to question, or political ascension. Indeed, I posit that there is often a good deal of apprehension in regard to emotionally strong, self-defining Black men, and I dare say, that the same holds true for Black women.

All things considered, the White male's psychological response is not that baffling to understand, considering the economic, educational and political progress Black people have made in this country. Understand that we were initially brought to America, in mass, to provide a free labor force, reproduce that free labor through our offspring, and continue slaving until we die. But after approximately two hundred fifty years of enslavement, we made if off the plantation and in due course, into economic, social and political realms that at the start, only a bold few earnestly imagined. What an amazing saga.

Let's review some history.

Race specific laws, and legally sanctioned brutality and punishment, began emerging in colonial America in the early 1600's.[83] The core motivation of which stemmed from racist thinking—Black people had dissimilar cultural roots and our physical appearance was much different from that of Whites, which was at the very least, visually discomforting. Many White men detested the idea of the Black male or female progressing economically and obtaining anything close to what they had. Hence, we have recorded events, such as what occurred in Wilmington, North Carolina in 1898; in Atlanta, Georgia in 1906; in Tulsa, Oklahoma in 1921; and Levy County, Florida (Rosewood) in 1923. Is it surprising that White supremacists are the top domestic terror threat/danger to us all? But what also prevailed as the White male's primary uneasiness, was the idea of Black males (this thing who in their estimation was less than fully human) being attracted to, and copulating with White women. As a result, lynching and genital mutilation began to take place. This was without doubt, due also in part to awareness that the genetic material of the Black male is genetically superior to that of the White male; resulting in a form of "penis envy".[84] It also seems quite plausible that White men feared that White women, by having intimate relationships with Black men, would become sympathetic to their circumstances, given the horrors that Black men suffered at the hands of White men. What could be more disturbing and terrifying than the thought that his woman might develop an emotional attachment to and begin cheering for the obvious underdog in the form of the demoralized and oppressed Black man? Thus, real or imagined sexual encounters involving a Black man and a White female routinely produced lethal results for the Black man.

In 1919, William Brown (a Black man) was seized by a mob from inside the Douglas Co. Courthouse in Nebraska after being "accused" of raping a White woman. He was stripped naked, beaten unconscious, shot, and dragged through the streets by an automobile. He was then hung on display from a downtown light pole.[85] Such were the atrocities repeated in towns across America.

From the 1600s until the civil rights movement in the 1960s, laws and regulations pertaining to interracial relationships were abundant and very eagerly enforced. Even when the laws began to change, Jim Crow ensured the continuation of "white justice," until after the conclusion of the civil rights movement.

That being said, White men adopted a different way of responding toward Black women, but with the same purpose, unquestionable control over them. In regard to the female he chose to exercise his self-designed authority and recognized liberty by doing to her what he pleased, sexually.[86]

Though he denied Black men access to his women by threat of death, he used, and sanctioned the use of the Black woman's body for unbridled sexual indulgence.

Such an approach must have been enormously gratifying in serving the White man's individual and collective ego, as the sexual exploitation of Black women was long condoned by legal practice and social norm.[87] As long as he could impetuously take and use at will the Black woman's most intimate possession (her vagina) he could easily conceptualize himself as being superior to the many strengths he saw in her. However, what started from the inclination of ego gratification and experiential fulfillment of identity rhetoric often produced a real emotional attachment and enduring feelings in response to the potency and beauty of feminine Blackness. Of course, this attraction during that time was concealed and publicly denied.

The third President of the United States, Thomas Jefferson, fits the aforementioned description quite well. The highly esteemed Mr. Jefferson fathered five children by his Black house slave, Sally Hemings. Their first child was born when Sally was only 17 years of age. Jefferson, though married to a White woman, maintained ongoing sexual activity with Ms. Hemings for years.

The dynamics of such interracial contacts are amazing to me in at least two aspects. The first is that despite their self-designated positions of racial superiority and social positions of advantage, many White men could not and cannot resist an attraction to the Black female, a phenomenon I refer to as the "Strom Thurmond Complex." Remember him? Mr. Thurmond was the late Senator from South Carolina who prided himself on being a "segregationist." After his death in June 2003, it was revealed that he, like Jefferson, had an ongoing sexual "relationship" with his black housemaid, with whom he also fathered a child. Of course, this little secret was not disclosed until after he was dead and buried.

Secondly, by history, the White man's concern of the Black male lusting for the White female appears to be evidence of a psychological phenomenon known as projection. That is, casting onto others what in actuality, you are emotionally experiencing yourself. The White male obviously saw the Black female as a desirable sex object, which by his behavior, he lusted after.

* * *

Traditionally, the White female's thinking about Black men and women was expected to reflect the mentality of her male counterpart, since generally, she was not permitted to openly think for herself. (It was her desire to free herself from this control that gave rise to the Women's Liberation Movement.) White men provided and promoted the script for her to follow. However, as with other duplicitous scripts provided in regard to cultural others, the script regarding the Black male was a con orchestrated to keep him at an extreme disadvantage and to distort the thinking of all concerning him. Blacks were generally depicted as cognitively inferior, naturally dirty, overly sexed, but also sexually undesirable.

All things considered, the White female could not have failed to notice the internal strength and resilience of Black men. She could not have mistaken what had been his self-discipline and humbled patience as nothing less than amazing forbearance. And so, although the Black male is often "feared" due still, to stereotyping produced by the fraudulent script, he is often simultaneously desired for his innate mental stamina, genetic dominance, and dark color. No doubt, White women will often "cross over" when the opportunity arises. From a Freudian perspective, she seeks to obtain what the White male does not have, that which contributes to his penis envy.[88] She makes her inner most desires quite plain when she speaks of finding a man who is tall, dark, and handsome.

Nor could the White female have overlooked the strength of person and effective mothering of the Black female. Mothering, not only in relation to the Black child born from the Black womb, but also in regard to the White children that often nursed from the Black breast. Hence, whether acknowledged or not, she knew the script was a sham. In consideration of the history and relational dynamics between the two, I deduce that the White female both envies and admires the Black female. Her admiration stems from her awareness of the innate strength of mind and spiritual authenticity possessed within the roots of Black womanhood, yet, she also envies the Black woman as the natural mate selection of the Black man. In addition, the White woman recognizes the enhancement of feminine beauty by darker skin color. They realize, as should we all, that the many hues of Blackness are indeed beautiful. Why else do so many spend the time, energy, and money to gain "deep, brown, beautiful tans," even while realizing that the lack of myelin in their skin substantially increases the danger of contracting skin disease and cancer from repeated exposure to the sun and/or tanning lights? It was reported that in 2009 alone, U.S. tanning salons generated revenues in excess of 5 billion dollars.[89]

Today, it is interesting that many American teens and young adults are in open rebellion against the dishonest scripts and hypocritical practices of their parents, grandparents, and great-grandparents. The younger generations especially, are readily and openly experimenting with interracial relationships like never before. Perchance, in some way, this will begin to remedy the racist orientation of some. However, in spite of this indication of script dismissal, the majority of the population continues to move away from honest and meaningful race related dialogue. We choose to see, speak, and hear no evidence of racism in the face of its continued presence around us. Hence, few of us are as psychologically and spiritually healthy as we are capable of being.

Until we reach the point of embracing, or at the very least accepting, each other's differences without the identified minority having to capitulate or mask his or her core differences to gain acceptance, we will remain relationally anemic. It is important that we respect different ethnic groups in ways that allow us to acknowledge the humanness of one another without offending, and to recognize our differences without impulsively becoming defensive. If presently, I have offended anyone, it was not intentional, but entirely consequential to my candidness.

CHAPTER SIX

The Science of Politics
(Ideologies at War)

> ALL ANIMALS ARE EQUAL
> BUT SOME ANIMALS
> ARE MORE EQUAL THAN OTHERS
>
> —George Orwell, Animal Farm, 1946[90]

The prerequisite for occupying political office within the D.C. beltway is having access to money—lots of money. Wealth is the mortar that maintains the well-constructed wall between the Washington politician and the average person. In our society, corporate, banking, and special interest financing work diligently to ensure that this wall is sustained because it is central to continuing status quo political activities that cater to the needs of the wealthy and the interest of big business. As a result, the typical citizen is unsympathetically misrepresented by today's politician, and the common person within the context of the American political structure often has little more than illusionary power to execute from within the voting booth.[91] The real life outcome is that those in the middle-class and below now desperately struggle to maintain their standard of living, if not to simply survive.

Census Bureau data for 2009 reported the highest rates of financial hardship in America since 1959.[92] These hardships have continued. It further reported that one out of every five children lives in poverty.[93] These numbers represent adults and kids living in the "land of the free and the home of the brave"—individuals who have been largely ignored and abandoned to their immediate conditions and circumstance; there are no lobbyists courting the Washington political incumbents on their behalf. Hence, the very selective attention of the Congressman and Senator is directed toward corporate giants and Wall Street executives, whose requests are not only heard, but legislatively granted. Subsequently, corporations zealously export jobs to foreign lands where labor is dirt cheap, the price of products and services are continuously raised to increase profit margins, CEOs slash jobs by the thousands while collecting millions of dollars in personal compensation, the cost of health care (again "big business") is permitted to escalate to the point of being immorally out of control, and the oil industry flaunts a level of greed that is so absurd that it defies suitable comment. Big business, big oil, and a financial/banking system gorge on the vulnerable masses, swelling their money coffers like never before in history. For certain, the best thieves rob you by sleight of hand. By the time you catch on, they are already making off with the goods.

No person living under the American flag, who is trying to play life fair and by the rules, should ever have to worry about making a choice between buying food, as opposed to having essentials such as medicine, housing, or heat in the winter. But with extremely lucrative corporations sheltering their wealth in off-shore accounts and avoiding U.S. taxes codes, along with the billions of taxpayer dollars financing two recent wars in the Middle East, money that should be put to constructive use to address critical domestic issues here at home has been unavailable. In view of the big picture, there is more than sufficient evidence to conclude that the average and poor person's welfare is not a priority to those who hold power in this country. As reported in 2010 United States Hunger and Poverty Facts and Statistics, "The operation of the U.S. political system, which should address the major problems of its citizens, is to a great extent not focused on fundamental concerns of poor people, whose ranks are ever-increasing, but on other concerns."[94]

Could it be possible that, sooner or later, an appreciable level of comfort and security will simply slip beyond the grasp of those even within the middle class? Do you find it interesting that those who fight the fiercest and speak most thunderously against meaningful reform to benefit the working class and poor are those who consider themselves pretty secure in life? For them, life sustaining necessities, services, and even pleasures, are taken for granted. They experience no personal anxiety about matters such as affording medical care or monthly groceries.

The masses will achieve fair-minded representation only when their political representatives come from their ranks—those who more closely reflect the reality of the average citizen. Today, as never before, we need real, well intentioned, *intelligent*, non-career minded politicians who are committed to those upon whose laboring backs America achieved its greatest prominence—the working class.[95] If we are to be a government of the people, by the people, and for the people, it is necessary that our political leaders be average, everyday hard working people; people who possess vastly more intelligence than many present day politicians give them credit.

But there is another essential criterion. We need leaders who highly honor humanity; that is, individuals who truly value human life, regardless of skin color, race, or ethnicity. Those who hold human interest, regardless of socioeconomic status or skin color to heart, and are not willing to sell out to greed, corporate America, special interest groups, lobbyists, or to one another for personal favors, immediate political endorsement, or career advancement. Otherwise, the majority of us—Black, White, and other—will continue to receive unfavorable representation and imbalanced effects. For instance, the current lean toward Medicaid, Medicare, and Social Security budget cuts will have detrimental consequences upon the working class and underprivileged, but it's considered an acceptable and necessary sacrifice by those in decision making positions who do not foresee themselves as ever having to rely upon these services for primary medical or supplemental monetary purposes. Yet, the same politicians advocating these changes resist adjusting the tax codes for the wealthiest populations who can very easily afford an increase in their tax expenditures.

* * *

The real "science" in political science lies in the ability of the powerful few to convince the masses to go against their own best interests. This is an extremely dismaying reality because, both historically and recently, the ideas and belief systems of the "few" eventually lead to massive death and destruction. No country has been or is immune.

Donald Trump has been a master mind, and very efficient, at convincing a certain segment of the population to work against their own best interest. How many have died in America due to mask wearing, and becoming vaccinated against the COVID-19 virus, becoming a political issue?

And when we consider "The Bush Doctrine," a wave of destruction and killing was launched in distant lands, beginning in Iraq and continuing in Afghanistan.[96] A by-product of this administrative endeavor was the depletion of America's treasury, the stripping away of certain civil liberties through the Patriot Act, and politically fed fear among the American people. Indeed, the many were led down a road that only a few had chosen.

Thousands of American soldiers and numerous U.S. citizens have died, been wounded, and disfigured in the Middle East since the beginning of our two recent wars. The death toll for American servicemen and women was far north of 6,000.[97] The number of deaths for Defense Department civilians was reported at 15.[98] In 2011, four days after researching the above death toll numbers for this text, 30 additional American servicemen were killed in Afghanistan after their helicopter was shot down by insurgents.[99] In addition, the casualty count among the Iraqi people alone has been estimated to be in the hundreds of thousands. In a mortality study conducted between 2002 and 2006 by Johns Hopkins University in collaboration with Al Mustansiriya University in Baghdad, the number of Iraqis killed since the start of the war was found to be in excess of 600,000.[100]

How "civilized" is a nation when it repeatedly resorts to violence to solve conflicts with differing ideological and religious cultures? America's two Middle Eastern wars speak to our restricted socio-intellectual and cultural orientation, which has persisted in this country since European explorers all but wiped out the native peoples on what were then "newly discovered" shores. At the time, America itself was considered "The New World". Today, the geopolitical climate suggests that what's past is indeed prologue to coming events.

Perhaps this is a leap in my thinking, but have you given much thought to the potentially dire consequences arising from the intercultural differences between Western/European society and other cultures during this era of globalization? Marimba Ani (2000) asks us to consider the Western mindset: "To Europeans, the universe represents actual physical space into which they can impose themselves."[101] And John Ikenberry (2002), an international affairs specialist, exposes the actual pursuits of those in power: "The new imperial grand strategy presents the United States [as] a revisionist state seeking to parlay its momentary advantages into a world order in which it runs the show." [102] He goes on to say that such activity causes lesser nations to "work around, undermine, contain and retaliate against U.S. power."[103]

In view of the historical record, many thousands may die as the collective Western/European ideological mindset seeks to achieve its ends, indeed, "The New World Order". If you've been following the international socio-economic and political climate of today, it is easy to conclude that we are moving toward an eventual climax of some sort. One must wonder if we are being set up for some mega-event prior to the unveiling of an ideological "solution" that will be very costly in human freedoms and lives—The Latin term, "Novus

Ordo Seclorum" or "New Order of the Ages," which appears on one of our most basic units of economic measure, the U.S. one dollar bill, seems to have extremely revealing significance regarding the efforts of the very powerful in the times in which we live.

But what will be the final outcome? What will be the culminating scenario in regards to the unending grasp for world supremacy and domination? Perhaps we are witnessing the progression toward the fulfillment of what will be prophetic words spoken by the late Dr. Martin Luther King Jr. who said, "We must either learn to live together as brothers, or we will perish together as fools."[104]

* * *

The political left stands against the political right, the Republican against the Democrat, the Progressive oppose the Conservatives, Trumpsters versus the liberals, and the haves against the have-nots. "War" is defined in *The American Heritage Dictionary* as "To be in an active state of conflict or contention."[105]

In addition to our foreign conflicts, war is occurring here on American soil. The battle lines have been drawn according to political views and ideological convictions. Because of deeply entrenched confrontational postures, little is achieved to remedy the issues of today. People are displaced from their homes (mortgage crisis), the economy remains weak (continued loss of jobs and employment), our children fall further behind in literateness (the educational crisis) and people die prematurely (lack of health care). We, the American citizens are the casualties of the ideological war.

How can our politicians speak of assisting and rebuilding other's countries when the health and welfare of so many people here at home are deteriorating before our very eyes? How can they purport to support democracy around the world, when there are such deep fissures in our own democratic institutions of government? Consider the recent fiasco regarding voting rights, or that leading to what became a last minute deal to raise the debt ceiling in response to the national debt.[106] It is time for warring ideologies to be laid aside and a cease-fire of divisive rhetoric declared. We need to stop warring with each other in order to address our pressing domestic needs beyond the superficial level that is endemic in today's politics. Would not a truly "civilized" culture worthy of global respect seek to impart a better quality of life to all her citizens?

Presently, selfish special interest groups are seeking to undo even the little progress made during the past few years. It has been called "taking back America," and is typically associated, in a derogatory manner, with the need for this "national retrieval." It is a movement largely driven by conservative Republicans and if successful, will impose a heavy toll particularly upon the working middle and lower classes.

I must ask, "Where is the protest?"

Except for that burst of political joie de vivre preceding the 2008 presidential election and BLM, I am amazed at how politically passive and socially inactive Black America as a whole has become. We are plagued by an apathetic conscience and lack of collective action, perhaps due to being desensitized by the many unending, often absurd politically related events continuously unfolding around us. I can only hope that there will be an awakening within our race, indeed an awakening within the entire country, which will spark a renewed drive for healthy political engagement and human equality.

Along with what was the October 2011 unveiling of the Dr. Martin Luther King monument in our nation's capital, I yearn for an unveiling of truth and an arousal of a moralistic national conscience.

CHAPTER SEVEN

A Response

Though there are individuals and groups, Black, White, and others, who apply their energy, talents and resources to assisting and improving the life circumstances of those in need, less fortunate, or who are victims of tragic events, the American way of life in general reinforces a manner of living that is individually focused (I, my, me), materially excessive, resource ravaging, and hedonistic. We are therefore at a point in our collective journey, where it is imperative for Black America to return to valuing family and community over the negative and self-centered influences of the broader society.

Many within the Black populace (young and old alike) have either inadvertently loss their foundational bearings regarding our heritage, or naively bought into the deception that our own traditions and historical philosophies regarding family, child rearing, reverence of older persons, and sense of community are inferior to those of the "majority" population. Consequently, many of "us" now exist in Black skin, absent that which has constituted the inner characteristics of admirable Black personhood. Such is the case when our family life, child rearing practices, communal pride, and esteem for one another no longer reflect qualities of respectability and mutual uplift; not to mention a faith oriented aplomb.

So I must ask, how do we, as a people regain our distinguishing beauty of character with legitimacy and distinction?

Although I certainly do not have all the answers, I offer a few suggestions that I believe will at least nudge us in the direction of reviving our withering roots of internal beauty. I will begin with Black men and young males—if it applies receive the feedback and embrace it:

- Those who are not doing so already, develop your mind. Earnestly challenge yourself intellectually. Develop your mind and pursue education as if were water to a thirsty man. Our cognitive abilities and minds are just as innately capable as all others; however, too often our intellectual and academic abilities are not sufficiently reflected in our actual performance, and our lives speak of wasted mental power. We/you have the capacity to change this.

- Do not get the essentials of manhood twisted. Real men stand on their own two feet. This doesn't mean that we don't or can't lean on our brother's shoulder in a moment of need, but with real men, the effort is toward accomplishment and maintaining ourselves in a productive position emotionally, mentally, financially, and relationally, so that we can act and think in terms of what is in our best interests and in the best interests of our women and children. I know there are many negative role models out there, but there are also an abundance of positive models as well. Consider what it is you are focusing on and make a change if necessary. Be ready to step away from the group when it is the right thing to do.

- When we as men procreate, we should make every effort to remain present and provide for the children we take part in producing. If we want the sex, then we should embrace the sacrifices that come along with child rearing. In other words, when that time comes to be a parent, be a man and fulfill your part. There are too many physically mature males who are still little boys mentally. We must afford our children the opportunity of growing up with the experience of what it is to have a present and caring father. If necessary attend a fatherhood course or parental training. The changes you can create in young lives will be substantial.

- Young brothers, stop maiming and killing one another. Stop ruining people's lives, people who are trying to survive. There is a higher calling for your life. Four or five generations ago your ancestors quite possibly lived on plantations not far from one another, if not together on the same plantation. Back then the only ones who did harm to their brothers or sisters were the ones, just like today, who could be counted on to sellout to some selfish motive—the weak minded and brainwashed.

- Gang-bangers, expand your minds! Think about this and think about it deeply—can there be a greater degree of self-generated mis-education and self-destructive mental programming than what you willingly subject yourselves to? You didn't invent the color that you claim allegiance to, nor did your contrived opponent invent the color to which he is aligned. It is an illusion, a cycle of deception, with palpable and often deadly consequences. Have you ever asked yourself: who owns the copyrights to a color? Crayola Crayons perhaps? And crayons are for kids! Let's explore a little further. You don't own the geographical location (turf) that you patrol and defend. You don't own the hood you represent. If the city, county, state, or federal government decides to take any area of your community to use for other means, you, your neighbor, and the old couple down the street will be moved out and relocated to places not even of your own choosing. It has happened many times before. Wake up! Recognize that the meaning of your life is greater than a street name, housing area, area code, gang symbol, or color. Do you know the actual roots of Black gang formation? It's more than standing around on a dark street corner at night carrying an illegal firearm, looking for an opportunity to prove your loyalty to a concept that robs you of your true identity and future. Understand that it is an imprisoned mind that keeps individuals caged in geographic spaces and underdeveloped mental places. If it's about the drug game, get out! Otherwise, you are living a predetermined life—selling dope, no hope, no future. It will be jail, the grave, disability, or, at best, old age with bitterness, stop settling for the lies you've been told or witnessed others living. Reclaim the true identity of who you are and live the life of a powerful Black man! Your predecessors were the first men to walk upright, the builders of pyramids, the inventors of the sciences, the rulers of kingdoms, and the possessors of creative and great minds. Yet you are willing to die for vice.

- Grown Black men, stop trying to be hip-hop and gangsta, denying the fact that you're over 30 years of age. Set an example for those younger brothers coming up behind you that will move them towards a deeper level of maturity.

- Young males, pull up your pants. People are tired of seeing the brand names of your underwear and/or the crevice of your behind. The whole appearance looks funky (literally). From a psychological perspective, I sometimes wonder if there is some subconscious (and perhaps not so subconscious) motive to drawing people's attention to your backside. What is the motive? Double earrings, braided hair, and attention to your behind. Do you even understand it?[107]

Ladies—if it applies:

- You don't have to get into bed with that male simply because he's telling you what you want to hear. What is he really showing you in terms of appreciating who you are and understanding who he is? Instead of going to bed with him to experience some fleeting sense of being loved and wanted, discover healthy love for yourself and go to bed each night with the dream of reaching your fullest potential in life. Awaken each day with a plan for transforming your dreams into reality. Every day, move a little closer to fulfilling your dreams. There is a whole world out there waiting for you to take a meaningful place in it.

- Ensure that your mind is developed. Make your intellect the focal point of men's (and other's) attention, not the size of your butt and breasts. Refuse to put yourself in the position of trying to love a man who only wants to use your body for semen disposal. You deserve more, but this is a reality that you must first realize and believe yourself.

- Ensure that your son is respectful of you and other females. Ensure that he has no reason to view you in a negative manner or depreciate you by who you associate or lay with. You mother will determine the mental imprint from which your son (and daughter) conceptualizes the opposite gender. So be careful of how you may spoil your child.

Males and females—if it applies:

- If you are a parent, love and rear your child to the best of your ability. Love and show love for your child. If the relationship between you and the other parent of your child has become unhealthy, then work something out that is in the best interest of the child. You worked together to produce the baby, you can work together to rear the child. And marriage, is still an honorable institution.

- Honor your heritage. Honor your mother. Honor your grandmother. Honor your father and your grandfather. Even though some of them have not actually earned that honor, honor them anyway. Honor them in how you talk and relate to them. For those who haven't earned it, tell them that you are moving beyond their issues, which in all honesty will require some of you to engage in some serious forgiving. But realize this, Forgiveness is good for the soul of the person doing the forgiving because it allows you to drop weighty emotional baggage and move on.

- Communally, we must lift our level of mutual respect for one another far above the ignominious terminology of "ho," "thug," "dog," and "bitch." We must highly esteem and value the opposite gender—we share the same roots! Understand that we desperately need to change the tone and substance of our male/female relations, so set a positive example. This will increase the chances that your own children will do the same.

- Respect your mind and body. Respect the mind and body of others. The Black community reportedly has the highest incidence of HIV infection in America. Regardless of how it originated, we cannot afford to play with our own lives or anyone else's. It you are sexually active and you have not already, learn you HIV status; get tested. Become real and significant to yourself. Become real and significant to others. A basic lesson of life is that others rarely value you above the degree you value yourself. Promiscuity can kill you.

- As parents, grandparents, aunts and uncles, older brothers and sisters, we have to become involved in the educational process of our young people. Take time to review homework assignments. Turn off the smart phone, television, gaming system, and iPod until homework is completed. It is incumbent upon us to create an intellectually rich and disciplined home environment. In addition, we should continuously demand increased public school funding, culturally relevant curricula, and in-school disciplinary measures that are conducive to our children's educational achievement and proper behavioral development. Let's find creative ways to make misbehavior in school a real learning experience, as unstructured home suspensions are simply a welcome respite for some. Unless we step forward and become more involved in our children's formal learning experience, our families and communities will continue to witness the Black child being disproportionately represented in dropout rates and poor academic performance. What's more, Black children (males in particular) will continue to be excessively labeled as "Intellectual Disability," "learning disabled," "emotionally disturbed," "severely emotionally disturbed," "ADD" (Attention Deficit Disorder), "ADHD" (Attention Deficit Hyperactivity Disorder), "ODD" (Oppositional Defiant Disorder), or "conduct disordered." As a result, those who are charged with educating our children will view them as being cognitively less capable, behaviorally dysfunctional, and/or mentally unbalanced. Worse still, some of these children will begin to welcome these labels as educational and behavioral crutches; i.e., ready made and socially acceptable excuses for being academically lethargic and/or inclined toward misbehavior. Thus, many will never develop their God-given intellectual and creative potentials to the fullest extent. Partner with other parents—there is still power in numbers. Get involved. Volunteer in your child's school. And though this requires sacrifice, it is a sacrifice with a payoff. Our children, our schools, and our communities will benefit.

- Teach the young the importance of earning honest money. But also teach them the importance of experiencing internal reward and satisfaction on a personal level, as we should not expect to receive monetary payment for everything we do.

- Become involved with your community's issues, as well as with local and national politics. Keep your eyes open and become aware of who is doing what. Understand why individuals and groups promote certain agendas. Look for the positive and what will be collectively beneficial, but also look for the hidden agendas, the prejudices, and the deceit.

- Let's pursue an ever-increasing depth and sincerity in our walk of faith, so that it again becomes the grounding force that promotes communal support and sparks actions exemplifying love and concern on behalf of others. The splendid truth of why we Black Americans kept getting up when knocked down and continued to achieve though perennially threatened by all sorts of external factors (troubled on every side), was because of our spiritual potency and the cooperative efforts coming from within our communities of faith. I sincerely believe our faith was more alive in times past than today. Though we see larger and more adorned churches, our presence, voices, and daily influence beyond the church walls and the designated day of worship have weakened. (For example, how did we ever permit prayer to be taken out of our schools?) Think about the Jamons (page 56-64) of this society and what they are interpreting from our actions.

CHAPTER EIGHT

My Concluding Thoughts

While going about your daily living, I encourage you to pause long enough to really pay attention to your inner voice. As you observe the immediate social issues and various world events of today, think about the potential impact of it all. Reflect upon it. Indeed, consider how your life is, or may be, affected by these occurrences; tune into your emotions and thoughts. Beyond this, take the time to ingest the adroit examination of reality as reflected in the words of an insightful minority poet. Listen to the depth of awareness contained in a well-developed Black sermon, as it examines faith's response to life events. And take note even, of the degree of social understanding spoken by that discerning individual at your local barber shop or beauty polar. Pause to listen, and if compelled, dare to speak. Share it as you see it.

Many of us have become quite skilled in the art of perceiving the core motives of people; that gut feeling that is an innate survival mechanism. It has served us well in times past. Today however, when it comes to that which works against us, we too often remain mostly inactive, unless we perceive some very imminent threat. More typically, we now choose to simply live with our awareness while grabbing hold to some sense of mental security within the confines of our communities, or, we aim to expend the greater part of our energy trying to obtain whatever we are allowed to have from those who possess the source of it.

* * *

I honestly believe that in many ways the course of integration severely weakened our Black identity, moral base, and collective drive. As we integrated, we steadily capitulated to a European world orientation and view of personhood. The subsequent deterioration of our broadly shared mutual support for one another and what was once recognized as shared behavioral boundaries followed; a process that weakened our communal role as a positive change agent within this society. Today, as we become increasingly culturally blended, the accompanying process of deeper behavioral and psychological merging with others threatens to exacerbate the attrition of what has been our own unique socially interactive record, as well as our emotional temperament and spiritual peculiarity. Unless we appropriately respond, we will continue to move further from the heritage that once nourished us with self-understanding and focused direction. In essence, our identity and guiding principles will fade away—Withering roots.

Were our customs and practices in the past less valid than that of the "majority" persons? Were our ways less effective in preparing us to develop an attitude of purpose, experiences of joy, and feelings of contentment? Some contemporary studies suggest that, in general, people are less internally satisfied today than they were a few generations or so ago, despite their increased wealth and material possessions.[108] Allow me to offer that real joy and contentment does not come from material possessions. It has its real basis in the spiritual realm.

Hence, once again, relevant questions turn out to be: "What is it that we are ultimately seeking and moving towards? Who are we becoming as a people? Are we adopting, or perhaps have we already irreversibly adopted, a Western mentality dominated by a focus on self (it's all about me), and material gain at the expense of others, the planet, and our souls?"

In his classic book entitled *The Souls of Black Folk*, W.E.B. Du Bois (1903), argued that the issue of color will be the major dilemma confronting American society in the 21st century.[109] How very accurate he was! However, looking at our present stance in society and the station of our existence, I wonder if Du Bois were to express his concern following an examination of his people in our present day, would he approach his composition from a different thematic perspective, and instead launch his discourse from the question, "What's to become of the souls of Black folk?"

The increasing loss, with each successive generation, of our time honored morals, values, and traditional wisdom beckons us to urgently reclaim those characteristics that have been integral to "our ways" for centuries. Practices and approaches to life that were once very prevalent, such as basic interpersonal manners being taught and extended to all, reverence for our elders, care for our babies, and cultivating the minds of our youth to be productive within our communities, towards our race, and broader humanity. Such culturally relevant norms and responsibilities are crying out for resurrection on a national scale.

To successfully accomplish this, we must reclaim a mindset that believes our traditional ideologies to be valid and worth preserving. A mindset that says our points of view have merit and that the voices of Black wisdom and strength of faith are more relevant today than ever before.

During the initial writing of this manuscript, the news media reported that three Black male adolescents entered a church in Richmond, California and shot two other Black male adolescents during a Sunday morning worship service. Such acts speak of youth who haven't a clue as to their personal value or culture. Be that as it may, it was further reported that only a few hours following these shootings, after the immediate investigation was complete and the police had departed the crime scene, the church members returned to their pews, the choir members went back into the choir stand, and the preacher re-entered the pulpit. Together, they resumed their worship service to its appropriate conclusion. In spite of tragic disruptions, and a period of delay, they returned to their proper places. Such is a demonstration of the faith, resiliency and determination that speaks to the deeper character of who we are as a people.

The first chapter of this book begins with poetry from the late great Black Renaissance poet Langston Hughes, who years ago wrote, "Beautiful . . . are the souls of my people." In closing, let me say that beautiful still are the souls of my people. So let us not compromise the truth, the essence, or the heritage of who we are. Let's retain the inner beauty of our personhood, so that "beauty" is not solely an outward physical appearance subject to diminishing with age. Instead, let's ensure that our beauty reflects a spiritual mainstay, and thus remains an applicable description in the beholding eyes of every observer who glances upon our presence and character, regardless of age or gender.

Where the internal beauty is lacking, let us rekindle it. Where it has disappeared, let us reclaim it. Let us allow the beauty of Blackness to come forth to sustain the hearts and minds of us as a people, individually and collectively. Let us then affect the hearts and minds of others for the betterment of society. Let us start by looking into the mirror at our individual selves, and making the necessary changes at a personal level. We can then set an immediate example and inspire our family members and those within our communities. If we achieve this, there can be no other outcome than inspiring and transforming the greater society.

The ills of our people and humanity await us.

CHAPTER NINE

Your Reflections

What then shall we say to this?
If God is for us, who is against us?

Romans 8:31

The final chapter is yours to compose. I invite you to note your own insights and thoughts regarding the matters I have presented, as well as any other events and experiences that are important within your own specified world. In addition, document what will be your self-mandated responsibilities and personal undertakings in response to your social and self-awareness, and dare to make a difference. Set a positive example for others. As you pursue this endeavor, converse with and challenge those within your inner circle and beyond. The final chapter is yours. Write and share it.

_____
_____
_____
_____
_____
_____
_____

ENDNOTES

Part 1

Notes:

[1] The Holy Bible, New International Version, *Ecclesiastes*, Chapter 1 verse 9 (Michigan: Zondervan, 1984).

Chapter 1

Notes:

[2] Langston Hughes, *Selected Poems of Langston Hughes* (New York: Alfred A. Knope, Inc., 1995) p. 13.

[3] Wade Noble quoted in Hunter Adams, *African Observers of the Universe*, in Journal of African Civilizations, 1979, Vol. I, No.2.

[4] Ted Sampley, *Barak Hussein Obama—Who is he?*, The U.S. Veteran Dispatch, December 29, 2006, Retrieved from *http://usvetdsp.com/dec06/obama-muslim. htm*; Internet. Also see, Philip Weiss, Who Is Barack Obama? And why do people say such loopy, ugly things about him? The enduring rot in American politics. New York News & Features, September 20, 2009, Retrieved from *http://nymag.com/news/politics/59265/*; Internet.

[5] For a thorough understanding of the historical relationship between Blacks on the African Continent and cultural others, the reader is referred to Chancellor Williams, The Destruction of Black Civilizations, Great Issues of a Race from 4500 B.C. to 2000 A.D. (Chicago, Illinois: Third World Press, 1987).

[6] Brandt Williams, The "n-word". Minnesota Public Radio, August 8, 2004, Retrieved from http://news.minnesota.publicradio.org/features/2004/06/28_williamsb_nword/.

[7] I believe that for some, the term nigga or nigger is anxiety provoking, at least mildly so, because of the negative mental associations (sometimes subconscious) derived from its historical use. Therefore, application of the word to self or others is avoided.

[8] Barbara Walters offended Sherri Shepard when she used the word "nigger" on the talk show "The View". At the time, the hosts were discussing the name (Niggerhead) previously identifying the hunting camp owned by the family of Governor Rick Perry. Though Whoopi Goldberg had also used the term within the context of the discussion, Sherri commented, "When white people say it, it brings up feelings in me." Should Barbra Walters have used the N-word? MSN TV News, October 3, 2011.

[9] I applaud the sisters who are going natural with their hairstyle. It speaks to an internalized confidence as to who you are, and to your inherent attractiveness.

[10] The Boondocks, is an American animated series created by Aaron McGruder for Adult Swim. The series premiered on

November 6, 2005, Retrieved from http://er.wikipedia.org/wiki/The_Boondoacks_(tv_series).

[11] Bill Bergstrom, "Ghettopoly" game called "racist": Blacks call for ban, boycott of Urban Outfitters, MSNBC News, October 9, 2003,

Retrieved from http:// www.msnbc.com/news/978212.asp.

[12] Dr. King and Malcolm X were the progenitors of a movement that they philosophically and religiously engaged from two different perspectives. Yet, they held the same intention and desired the same outcome—to permanently raise the self-respect of, and society's esteem for, black human beings and others who are often marginalized and handicapped by social and economic challenges. The reader is encouraged to read Jules Archer, They Had a Dream: The Civil Rights Struggle from Frederick Douglass to Marcus Garvey to Martin Luther King and Malcolm X, (New York: Penguin Books USA Inc., 1993).

[13] I have wondered how certain influential and great personalities of the past would respond to contemporary society. Here I offer an imagined conversation between Dr. M.L. King Jr. and Malcolm X.

[14] Mark Rahner and Jennifer Sullivan, Teen beaten in transit tunnel; Metro reviews policies, The Seattle Times, February 9, 2010.

[15] Ibid.

[16] See http://specials.msn.com Teens—arrested in Kidnapping, assault, Retrieved February 1, 2011.

[17] I have spoken to groups of young black males about this issue and have very frequently received this response: "If I don't know you, it's none of my business what happens to you." Some will even go so far as to say, "I don't care nothing about you if I don't know you."

[18] Patrick Buchanan, The Beltway Sniper and the Media, The American Cause, October 30, 2002, Retrieved fromhttp://www.theamericancause.org/patthebeltwaysniper.htm.

[19] Recall the recent case in 2010 of Amy Bishop.

[20] A short article entitled Evaluating a psychological profile of a serial killer, sheds insight into the historical profile of these individuals, Retrieved from www.uplink.com.au/lawlibrary/Documents/DOCS/DOC5.html.

[21] 9 dead in shooting at Connecticut beer distributor, Union Official: Gunman was employee who had been caught stealing, Associated Press, August 8, 2010, Retrieved from http://www.msnbc.msn.com/id/38535909.

[22] Jeff Gardere explores this issue in his article entitled, Did Racism Fuel the Omar Thornton Work Place Massacre? BLACKVOICES, August 9, 2010, Retrieved from http://www.bvblackspin.com/2010/08/09/did-racism-fuel-the- omar-thorton-work-place-massacre/.

Chapter 2

Notes:

[23] Definition of Kesserian ingera, Retrieved October 2010 from http://www. definition-of.com/Kasserian+Ingera.

[24] The reader is referred to Albert Bandura, Social Learning Theory, (New York: General Learning Press, 1977). Also see Julian B. Rotter, The development and application of social learning theory, (New York: Praeger, 1982).

[25] NFL's Vick Indicted on Charges of Dog Fighting, NPR, July 18, 2007, Retrieved from http://www.npr.org/templates/story/story.php?storyId=12 104472.

[26] Illegal Dog fighting Rings Thrive in U.S. Cities, NPR, July 20, 2007, Retrieved from http://www.npr.org/templates/story/story.php?storyId=12 104472. Also see Dog fighting in the United States, Wikipedia, the free encyclopedia, Retrieved from http://en.wikipedia.org/wiki/Dog_fighting_in_the_United_ States.

[27] John B. Watson, Behaviorism (New York: Guilford Press, 1930) p. 82.

[28] On "Good Morning America", December 10, 2003, a special news segment revealed the disruptive and increasing aggressive behaviors of children in Kindergarten.

[29] Allen Levine, Angela Chambers and Imaeyen Ibange, Third Grader at Center of Teacher Attack Plot Speaks, Good Morning America, April 7, 2008, Retrieved from http://abcnews.go.com/GMA/AsSeenOnGMA/story?id=46 02938.

[30] Edecio Martinez, Michael Brewer New Pictures: Teen's Remarkable Recovery After Being Set on Fire, CBS News, March 23, 2010, Retrieved from http://www.cbsnews.

com/8300-504083_162-504083.html?keyword=boy+burned+by+bullies.

[31] 14-YEAR-OLD-BOY SHOOTS FATHER, Inside edition, April 22, 2010, Retrieved from http://www.insideedition.com/news/4356/14-year-old-boy- shoots-father.aspx.

[32] http://www.9news.com/video/1103351219001/0/3-siblings-arrested-after-high- speed-chase-shootout.

[33] http://www.msnbc.msn.com/id/44108677/ns/local_news-nashiville_tn/t/memphis-police—year-old-student-planned-advance-kill-principal/.

[34] Rosemary Bennett, Gangs replace parents as role models for troubled teens, The Sunday Times, August 8, 2010,

Retrieved from

www.timesonline.co.uk/tol/news/uk/crime/artcle4481517.ece. See also Youth gangs no longer just a big city problem, CNN, April 23, 1997, Retrieved from http://www.cnn.com/US/9704/23/gangs/index.html.

[35] Blacks continue to be incarcerated at a higher rate than whites, even for the same or similar crimes.

[36] Brian A. Primack, Erika L. Douglas, Michael J. Fine & Madeline A. Dalton, Exposure to Sexual Lyrics and Sexual Experience Among Urban Adolescents, American Journal of Preventive Medicine, Volume 36, Number 4. 2009.

[37] Ibid.

[38] For an in depth understanding, see Marimba Ani, YURUGU, AN AFRICAN-CENTERED CRITIQUE OF EUROPEAN

CULTURE THOUGHT AND BEHAVIOR, (Trenton, New Jersey: African World Press, Inc., 2000) p. 279-308.

[39] Ibid. pp. 311-335.

[40] Definition of Kesserian ingera, Retrieved October 2010 from http://www. definition-of.com/Kasserian+Ingera.

Chapter 3

Notes:

[41] Arnold Adoff, The Poetry of Black America: Anthology of the 20th Century, (New York: Harper & Row, 1973) p 250.

[42] Gerald C. Ogbuju, Absent Fathers: its impact on the family, May 2008, Retrieved from http://www.onlinenigeria.com/articles/ad.asp?blurb=645.

[43] The overall "self-image" is often negative, with little real confidence in one's abilities outside of some very strict parameters. In regards to the core ideas related to "manhood", one's cognitive distortions and faulty belief systems must be addressed.

[44] The use of the black stud and the sexual behavior of the slave master towards the female slave manifestly demeaned the emotional and physical relevance of those in captivity. The reader is invited to read Devin A. Robinson and Verno Roper, *Blacks: From The Plantation to the Prison*; (Atlanta, Georgia: Going Against The Grain Publications. 2008) p. 22-24.

[45] A psychological occurrence called "generalization."

[46] Aside from my clinical experience, my thinking was also informed by Earl Ofari Hutchinson, *Black Fatherhood: the*

guide to male parenting, (Los Angeles: Impact Publication, 1992).

[47] Franklin B. Krohn and Zoe Bogan, *The effects fathers have on female development and college attendance,* College Student Journal, December 2007.

[48] Ibid.

[49] Erol Ricketts, *The Origin of black female-headed families,* p.34. Retrieved from

http://www.irp.wisc.edu/publications/focus/pdfs/foc121e.pdf.

[50] *Black Women Students Far Outnumber Black Men at the Nation's Highest-Ranked Universities,* The Journal of Higher Education, April 1, 2006.

[51] Earl Ofari Hutchinson, *Black fatherhood: the guide to male parenting,* (Los Angeles: Impact Publishing, 1992) p. 71.

[52] Napoleon Bryant, Jr., *African American Males: Soon Gone?,* Journal Of African American Studies, Vol.4, Number 4, p.9.

[53] Linda Malon-Colon, *Responding to the Black marriage Crisis: A New Vision for Change,* Research Brief No. 6, Future of the Black Family Series, June 2007.

[54] There is a good deal of controversy surrounding this issue, as to whether a two parent opposite gender family system provides any significant benefit over an attentive single parent or same sex family system. My personal thinking is grounded within a Christian perspective in regard to what I offer here as being ideal. This does not negate certain other arrangements, as life events occur that often prevent the

ideal; however, I do believe that when we purposely move beyond the natural arrangement within the male-female relational design, we invite increased opportunity for eventual undesirable outcomes at an emotional and spiritual level. My thinking is also partially influenced by Paul Petit, *Dynamic Dads*, (Wheaton, ILL, 2003), and Margaret Meeker, *Strong Fathers, Strong Daughters*, (Washington, D.C., Regency Publishing, 2006).

[55] The reader is referred to Sampson Davis, George Jenkins, and Rameck Hunt, THE PACT, (New York: Penguin Group Inc., 2003), The authors provide their real life story of being three black male youth with absent fathers who make a pact with each other to pursue their educational goals to become medical doctors. All three succeed. They also authored, *THE BOND*, (New York: Penguin Group INC., 2007). Here they share their individual efforts to reconnect with there fathers after attaining adulthood.

[56] The social and familial histories of most delinquent and/or confined youth are very similar—The "specified worlds" that John B. Watson (1870-1958) spoke about. In regard to the adolescent I am naming as Jamon (not his actual name), I provided individual counseling/therapy for approximately two and a half years.

[57] Incarcerated Juveniles will sometimes purposely postpone their discharge from confinement because the protection and safety they feel while incarcerated far exceeds what they experienced within their homes and communities.

[58] By "our" own children, I am speaking in the collective sense to include those within and outside our individual households.

59 It was the time of "Say it loud, I'm Black and I'm proud!"

Chapter 4

Notes:

60 The Schott 50 State Report on Black Males & Education; Retrieved October 31, 2010 from http://www.blackboysreport.org.

61 TiAja Elllis, Are Black male High School Drop Out Rates Hurting America, August 30, 2010, Retrieved from http://www.Suite101.com/content/are-black- male-high-school-drop-out-rates-hurting-america—a280321.

62 Ibid.

63 Ibid

64 The reader can learn more about the particular program by visiting, http:// www.theprovidenceeffect.com.

65 Ibid.

66 Jawanza Kunjufu, Countering The Conspiracy To Destroy Black Boys, (African American Images, 1985) p. 23.

67 Ibid. p.7-32

68 Poll: Most Americans see lingering racism in others, CNN U.S., December 12, 2006, Retrieved from http://articles.cnn.com/2006-12-12/us/racism.poll_1_whites-blacks-racism?_s=PM:US.

69 My argument is based upon the observation that little, in recent years, can be identified as a well led effort to counter racism. Because White America typically fail or refuse to see

racism as a problem, the broader media and resources cannot be counted upon to assist in remedying it.

[70] Tim Craig and Michael D. Shear, *Allen Quip Provokes Outrage, Apology*, The Washington Post, Tuesday, August 15, 2006.

[71] Ibid.

[72] www.digitaljournal.com/article/3039905

[73] Don Imus, Rush Limbaugh, Pat Buchannan and Senator Harry Reid, just to name a few; and surprisingly, we also heard former president Bill Clinton make the statement that the then presidential candidate Barack Obama ". . . would be serving us coffee a few years ago."

[74] October 31, 2011 Fox News

[75] Poll: *Most Americans see lingering racism in others*, CNN U.S., December 12, 2006, p.1, Retrieved from http://articles.cnn.com/2006-12-12/us/racism.poll_1_whites-blacks-racism?_s=PM:US.

[76] Rakesh Kochlar, Richard Fry & Paul Taylor, *Wealth Gaps Rise to record Highs Between Whites, Blacks, Hispanics-Twenty-to-One*, Pew Research Center, July 26, 2011.

[77] The Associated Press, Fired from NPR, Williams Begins Bigger Role on Fox, October 23, 2010, Retrieved from http://www.npr.org/templates/story.php?story.phpId=130719463.

[78] Ibid.

[79] Unlike the still controversial 2000 election of George Bush Jr., that required Supreme Court intervention before he was

officially recognized as the newly elected President of the United States.

[80] Oscar Avila, *Obama's census choice: Simply African-American*, Chicago Tribune, April 2, 2010. Also see Sam Roberts and Pater Baker, *Asked to Declare His Race, Obama Checks 'Black'*, New York Times, April 2, 2010. Such were the head lines throughout the nation, and indeed the world.

[81] Ibid

[82] Michael D. Shear, *Obama Defends 'Limited' Role in Libya*, The Caucus, March 28, 2011.

[83] A. Leon Higginbotham, Jr., *IN THE MATTER OF COLOR: Race & The American Legal Process: The Colonial Period*, (New York: Oxford University Press, 1980) p. 19-60.

[84] For an interesting read on the issue of White male's "penis envy" the reader is referred to Dr. Frances Cress Welsing, *THE ISIS PAPERS: THE KEYS TO THE COLORS*, (Washington: C.W. Publishing 1991) p. 93-101.

[85] Carson Clayborne, *Civil Rights Chronicle: The African American Struggle for Freedom*, (Lincolnwood, Illinois 2003) P.56.

[86] The reader is referred to Katie Geneva Cannon, Katie's Canon: Womanism and the Soul of the Black Community, (New York: Continuum 1996) p.49. Katie, a Christian womanist theologian, also provides an intriguing discussion of the White woman's response to Black womanhood, p. 73. The way in which I view the White female as following, "the script' in what I present in this chapter, requires a psychological occurrence such as presented by Katie.

[87] Today, Black females are most often raped by Black men. Sadly, many Black men have adopted or inherited a low estimation of the Black woman. Even when not raped in the literal sense, the Black female is often sexually exploited (raped) in the figurative sense—music videos, song lyrics, literature.

[88] Again the reader is referred to Dr. Frances Cress Welsing, *THE ISIS PAPERS: THE KEYS TO THE COLORS*, (Washington: C.W. Publishing 1991) p. 93-101.

[89] Dan Wright, *Working The Tan—Tanning Salons Grow*, The Daily News Record, (Harrisonburg, VA) September 11, 2009.

[90] George Orwell, *Animal Farm*, (New York: Harcourt Brace Jovanovich, Inc., 1946; reprint ed., Alfred A. Knope, Inc. 1993) p. 88. George Orwell creatively depicts the nature of domestic politics through a fictional story involving the interactive behavior and character of animals on a farm.

Chapter 5

Notes:

[91] I use the term "illusionary" because currently America seems to be on a fairly steady course toward political and economical self-destruction regardless of which political party is managing the operative agenda. Increasingly, the real seat of power is revealed to lie within the financial arena.

[92] *Half in Ten says to act now*, The Richmond Voice, Vol.24, No. 401 (1195th Edition) September 29-October 5, 2010. p.2.

[93] Ibid.

⁹⁴ *2010 United States Hunger and Poverty Facts and Statistics,* Retrieved from

http://www.worldhunger.org/articles/Learn/us_hunger_facts.htm.

Chapter 6

Notes:

⁹⁵ I italicized intelligent in this sentence because currently, intelligence does not always appear to be a highly valued trait within the political arena. There are those today, drawing huge crowds of followers, who demonstrate very little depth of thinking. I am not sure if it's more about simply having a certain look or the right sound bite, but the fact that so many can be drawn into the inanity of shallow charades is perplexing.

⁹⁶ Dale T. Snauwaert, *The Bush Doctrine and Just War Theory,* The Online Journal of Peace and Conflict Resolutions 6.1 Fall: 121-135 (2004). Retrieved from *www.trinstitute.org/ojper/6 1snau.pdf.*

⁹⁷ Defense Department

⁹⁸ Ibid.

⁹⁹ *30 Americans die in downing of helicopter,* The Richmond Times dispatch, Sunday, August 7, 2011. p.1

¹⁰⁰ Gilbert Burnham, Shannon Doocy, Elizabeth Dzeng, Rijadh Lafta & Les Roberts, *The Human Cost of the War in Iraq: A Mortality Study,* John Hopkins University, Baltimore & Al Mustansisiya University, Bagdad, 2006).

101 Marimba Ani, *Yurugu; An African-Centered Critique Of European Cultural Thought And Behavior*, (Trenton; African World Press, Inc., 2000) p.490.

102 John Ikenberry, *Foreign Affairs*, September-October 2002.

103 Ibid.

104 Speech in St. Louis Missouri, March 22, 1964.

105 The American Heritage Dictionary, 2nd College Edition, (Boston; Houghton Mifflin Co., 1985).

106 US Congress narrowly votes to raise debt limit - BBC News, December 15, 2021, retrieved from https://www.bbc.com

107 I have often wondered if this presentation among our Black males is a direct correlate to the depletion of strong male role models, as double earrings, braided hair, and fashions giving attention to the back side of one's body contour has typically been a feminine practice.

108 Zhou Zheng, *Are Modern People Happier than People Who Lived in the Past*? PureInsight.org, Retrieved November 27, 2010 from *www.pureinsight.org/ node/3990*.

109 W.E.B. Du Bois, *The Souls of Black Folk*, (New York: Bantam Books, 1989). Du Bois first published this book in 1903

ABOUT THE AUTHOR

Dallas T. Lee earned a Master of Science degree in Clinical Psychology from Radford University. He has also earned a Master of Divinity degree from Virginia Union University, Samuel Dewitt Proctor School of Theology. Dallas has worked with emotionally disturbed adolescents and their families for nearly 30 years. He and his wife have reared 3 children. They have been married for 33 years.

Altered Compass invites you into dialogue that explores social dynamics at play within the American culture that speak to a transforming identity, as pertaining to Blackness.

www.ingramcontent.com/pod-product-compliance
Lightning Source LLC
LaVergne TN
LVHW012109070526
838202LV00056B/5683